THE
FOUNDER'S
TALE

THE FOUNDER'S TALE

A GOOD IDEA
AND A GLASS OF MALT

PIP HILLS

BIRLINN

First published in Great Britain in 2019 by
Birlinn Ltd
West Newington House
10 Newington Road
Edinburgh
EH9 1QS

www.birlinn.co.uk

ISBN: 978 1 78027 628 1

British Library Cataloguing-in-Publication Data
A catalogue record for this book is available on request from
the British Library

Typeset by Initial Typesetting Services, Edinburgh
Printed and bound by Clays Ltd, Elcograf S.p.A.

For Maggie

Contents

Preface

A friend reported this conversation, which took place some years ago in the Abbotsford Bar in Edinburgh's Rose Street. Three men, deep in conversation, are drinking pints of ale. The first is telling a story about Pip Hills. When he has finished, the second man asks: 'Who is this Pip Hills I keep hearing about? Is he famous?' The third man says, 'Famous? No, he's not famous.' Then, thoughtfully, 'He's better than that: he's legendary. He's the sort of guy people tell stories about in pubs.'

For those readers who don't drink in Scottish pubs and consequently know nothing about me – me not being famous – perhaps I should tell you something of what this book is about. It has quite a lot to do with stories in pubs. I think the main difference between public houses and other sorts of hostelries is that the former are, above all, places where people tell stories about their friends and acquaintances. And since no storyteller worth his or her salt will diminish the dramatic content of a story, legends are born, and propagated, and the mundane becomes, by a gradual process, the heroic. This I know, because over the years I have heard stories told about my friends – and sometimes about myself – and I have watched the tales grow. On the whole, the embellishments which a story accrues are improvements; but not always, for the motives of the tellers are as varied as the tellers themselves.

The Founder's Tale has to do with stories of this sort: it's about something I did many years ago, with the help of some of my friends. It's a story which has grown in the telling, until

I sometimes have difficulty in recognising the original. So I decided that while I was still this side of eternity, maybe it would be a good idea to set down the events as I saw them. I don't pretend that this is the only true account – for recollection is always selective – but it is as I saw it. And it's not just about me; for I was happy in my friends, who were often the sort of folk who themselves became legendary, and the story contains stories about them. Alas, I have had to omit some of the best stories, out of respect for the law – but that can't be helped.

The main story, though, is about the founding of the Scotch Malt Whisky Society, and my part in that. It is an unusual institution: not so unusual now as it was when it began, for it has had many imitators, though none which carry its happy freight of stories – or offer its members quite such excellent liquor. I think the nature of the Society will become apparent in what follows, so there is no need to tell you about it here. And of course, if you are already a member, no doubt you have heard some of the stories already. I assume the mantle of the horse's mouth (to mix a couple of metaphors), so you can say you had it from there.

Pip Hills
Montrose
August 2019

CHAPTER 1

A Field of Barley

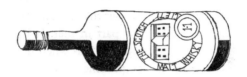

Because the beginnings of the Scotch Malt Whisky Society go back a long way it is sometimes tempting to ask: if this or that had or hadn't happened, how different would things have been? It is, by and large, an unprofitable kind of speculation, but tempting nonetheless. For example, if K's grandfather hadn't gone pearl fishing in the Torres Strait, I don't suppose she and Duncan would have had the wherewithal to buy their little farm. And I wouldn't have gone to visit, and we wouldn't have mowed the barley, and I would never have met Stan. And if I hadn't met Stan, I might never have had the least interest in whisky. I should explain.

Duncan is one of my oldest and dearest friends: our paths first crossed nearly sixty years ago. He is a quiet man who, without trying, is distinguishable from his neighbours in several ways, only some of which they are aware of. He still speaks with the soft lilt of his native Easter Ross, which is very different from the heavy Doric of Aberdeenshire. And, of course, he has a PhD in prehistoric archaeology, which comes in handy now and then. A good man to know if your digger unearths a

1

pile of bones. K, too, had an extensive and expensive education, but neither of them is impressed by such things and back in the seventies they decided against academic careers in favour of breeding garrons. The garron is Scotland's indigenous horse: not very tall but very strong and good at climbing hills. You can see pictures of them on some of the stones which the Picts carved more than a thousand years ago.

When they bought Denmill Farm that summer, it was in a very decrepit state, with fields of standing crops and huge piles of rusting farm machinery. (For those who don't know about such things, I should say that farm machinery is one of the few relics of the glory days of mechanical engineering before Health and Safety. There are lots of fast-moving bits and if you get in the way, you lose pieces of your body.) Shortly after they took possession of the farm, I naturally showed up: out of a desire to help, but mainly from curiosity. It had been a fine summer and the barley was ready for mowing.

Duncan showed me around, knowing I shared his liking for old machines. The most prominent thing in the yard was a vast and ancient device which Duncan said he reckoned was a combine harvester. He needed a harvester of some kind if the barley was to be brought in, and the good weather was forecast to end a few days later. We inspected the machine. Viewed as a whole, it was incomprehensible, but if you looked closely, you could get some notion of what – maybe – various parts did. Obviously, the thing to do was to get it going and see what happened. The motive power was apparently a diesel engine, low-set and very rusty. Happily by that time my life-long relationship with diesels had begun and I could report that, since all the injectors were in place, it might well be viable. Also, it was a 2.2 litre BMC, a dull, if worthy, workhorse, for which spares would be available from the local scrap dealer. So, while I fettled the engine, Duncan squirted oil into every joint, and after a couple of hours we were ready to have a go.

We borrowed a tractor battery and fired the thing up. It ran as sweetly as we could wish, if somewhat dirty in the exhaust. Duncan climbed aboard and I stood well back. He tried various wheels and levers and, after a bit, Leviathan stirred and then moved slowly forward. One lever raised the cutter bar; another set the elevator going; a third, screeching, activated the innards. That evening he drove the harvester slowly through the gate into the barley field and there we left it. K had found a pile of sacks and some bales of binder twine in a byre, so we were equipped.

Early the next morning we set the machine to the barley. The crop was fully ripe and bone-dry. Duncan's progress was slow and very erratic; but the machine cut the barley stalks; it threshed them and it winnowed them and it spat the barley grains into the sacks. By ten in the morning the whole valley knew that those townies up at Denmill were trying to mow barley with a machine which their predecessors had abandoned long ago. By eleven there were Land Rovers and tractors parked in the road and delighted spectators leaning on gate or fence to view the most amusing thing the Howe of Alford had seen in years. Fingers would point at the wavy lines of stubble which Duncan was leaving behind him – for those were people for whom straightness of furrow was second only to money in the bank. The merriment continued all that day, causing serious congestion on the road. From time to time a driver, wrathful at being unable to pass, would, on being shown the cause, join in the jollity, thereby increasing the blockage.

All that long day, under looming clouds, Duncan, perched high on his harvester, continued to make his wandering way up and down the field while I, driving the tractor, ferried sacks of barley from field to barn. As evening was falling he parked the machine in the yard and we wrestled the last of the heavy – but perfectly dry – sacks up on to their stack. At that point it started to rain. It rained all night and all of the next day. In

3

fact it scarcely stopped raining for nearly six weeks and crops rotted in the ground. Duncan and K had the only harvest in the Howe that season, and a lot of people who had been laughing over the gate began to wonder whether perhaps the townies knew something they didn't.

It may not be immediately apparent what this has to do with the Scotch Malt Whisky Society, but it fell out as follows. As a consequence of the affair of the barley field, my friends' standing in the valley was perceptibly improved. They had, after all, the best part of a thousand pounds' worth of barley in the barn while everyone else was looking at a substantial loss. The difference in attitude was apparent wherever a few were gathered together and some even came calling, in a social sort of way. Of the latter, none was more welcome than Stan, whose farm ran contiguous to Denmill. Stan had a big arable farm and was a wealthy man by any reasonable standard. Being an Aberdeenshire farmer, his wealth was apparent neither in his speech nor in his dress – nor in his dwelling, which was a little, two-storey farmhouse on the side of a hill. It was evident in his cattle, though: a large herd of glossy Herefords, any one of which could have graced the Royal Highland Show with little notice.

Stan appeared to take a liking to me although – or possibly *because* – our views on just about everything differed so greatly. He was mystified that I should be content to have two lovely daughters and no desire for any more children. 'Hae awa wi' the quines, man, and breed a loon,' he would say, though without any undue machismo. When I visited, as I have done a few times a year since then, the grapevine would do what grapevines do, and Stan would appear of an evening, bearing a lemonade bottle full of a dark liquid, ready for a few hours' discussion of politics, philosophy and economics. On matters social and political, we were as far apart as Achiltibuie and Alpha Centauri, but we did concur where the contents of the

4

bottle were concerned. For the bottle held whisky, which Stan drank neat and I with a dash of tap water.

It was without doubt the finest whisky I had ever tasted (not that I could have been said to be a connoisseur of whisky – or of anything else, for that matter, save perhaps diesel engines), and was unlike anything I had drunk before. I had grown up, a Scot among Scots, in a house in which there was always a bottle of whisky, but this was kept as a ritual offering to visitors and was not for domestic consumption, for the only thing my father drank was Hollands gin, and little enough of that. (I don't suppose that in thirty years there was ever a bottle of genever in our house which had duty paid on it, but that's another story.) Our household whisky was always Haig or Bell's or the like, and by my late teens I had decided I didn't care for the stuff. Beer was what young men drank then and I didn't like that much either. (Real ale had yet to make its appearance.) So Stan's whisky was a bit of a revelation. Not only did it taste amazing, but we could polish off the best part of a bottle in an evening and in the morning, while I could not be said to be a well man, I would be content to be alive – which was not commonly the case, for I have long suffered from the sort of hangovers in whose depths suicide seems an attractive option.

After a few episodes of this sort, I enquired of Stan where he got the whisky, and he told me. Once a year he would get into his old Land Rover and drive up over the Cabrach Pass and down into the valley of the Spey. When he got to the river, he would turn left and head up the valley to Ballindalloch, where from George Grant at Glenfarclas distillery he would buy a quarter cask of mature whisky. Glenfarclas had long made a practice of maturing a small amount of their malt spirit in sherry quarters, which they would sell in the cask to regular customers. 'Regular customers' gives the wrong impression here, suggesting as it does someone who buys his or her newspaper from the same shop every morning. A customer for one of those casks was generally someone whose father had bought a cask once a year, and his father before him, and so on. It was a system of supply which you couldn't buy into with mere money, you had to inherit your place. It was probably a relic of a time when glass bottles were uncommon and one bought whisky either in a jug or – if you were wealthy enough – in a cask.

A quarter cask fitted rather nicely into the back of an old Land Rover and Stan would take his cask home to his little farmhouse. There he would start the bung and replace it with a brass spigot. The cask he would lodge on a specially-made wooden stand and, sitting in an old brown leather armchair by the fire, he would draw himself a dram. He was a happy man.

CHAPTER 2

A Good Idea,
a Party and a Syndicate

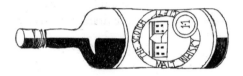

In those days I had a great many friends in and around Edinburgh and to most of them I told the story of the amazing whisky. The tale improved in the telling, as such things do, and the idea emerged that I should enquire whether there were any chance of getting hold of such a cask, with the intention of asking my chums to share it. At that stage I knew nothing of what it would cost, or whether any would be procurable, or why it was so fine. It was a good idea and it had all the characteristics of a *good idea*, namely that everyone agreed as to its excellence and none of us had the slightest idea how to make it happen. But there was no harm in trying, so off I set on a wave of optimism for the Howe of Alford, to enquire as to the possibility of buying a cask of whisky.

It is perhaps worth remarking at this point that by the later 1970s, most folk in Scotland had no idea of the difference between malt and blended whiskies. Whisky was a *good thing* and you drank it neat, preferably with a chaser of strong ale. This was a very efficient way of getting very drunk in a very short time – and for most of my fellow Scots, that's what whisky was for. Single malts were little-known in Scotland and almost totally unknown anywhere else. A few independent distillers bottled some of their product as a single malt, but very few. As far as the industry was concerned, such people were just a nuisance, distracting attention from the supposed excellencies of the blended stuff.

Happed comfortably in my ignorance, off I went to Denmill and, as usual, Stan came over for a chat. Before the drams had had too much effect, I explained what I was about. He was very helpful, telling me what his last cask had cost him, and happy to let me have the Grants' phone number. Furthermore I was welcome to use his name, he being a customer of very long standing. I called Glenfarclas and enquired as to the possibility of buying one of their fine sherry quarters. I was in luck: one of their customers had recently died and had inconsiderately left no one to inherit his annual cask. Stan's recommendation carried weight, indicating that I was a serious and respectable person, despite being a lowlander. I went hotfoot back to Edinburgh and spoke to those of my friends who had expressed an interest in joining with me in the pursuit of the *good idea*. This was in the autumn of the year. I had enough prospective participants for us each to have about a gallon of the malt (which seemed a rational quantum of whisky) if the contents of the ten-year-old cask were to turn out as expected.

Just about then Frances Gordon announced her intention of throwing a sherry party. Frances was an elegant, intellectual old lady who lived at the other side of the square. (We both inhabited what, confusingly for outsiders, is called Edinburgh's New Town – it was new in 1760.) She had a beautiful Georgian apartment full of lots of ancient rugs and some very fine eighteenth century mahogany furniture. (One of the rugs is beside me as I write: a blue-ground Kazakh.) At Frances' sherry parties I acted as butler, pouring drinks and chatting to her guests, who were mostly very much older than I was. Another of my functions was to polish the glasses before we served the drinks, a duty I took seriously. The glasses, a miscellaneous lot, were kept in a cabinet made in Napoleon's day, which was infested with woodworm. Besides polishing each glass, I was able to remove the little brown woodworm beetles. Frances never noticed them, though I suspect her guests did, if one escaped my scrutiny and was served up swimming in Amontillado.

It was at one of Frances' previous parties that I had first met Ritchie Calder. Ritchie was undoubtedly one of the good and the great, though not by desire and he carried it lightly. It's a bit difficult to tell you in a few words what an amazing guy Ritchie was. He had had a long career as a radical journalist and in 1941 had been shanghaied into the Political Warfare Executive, an outfit that was shadier than MI6 and probably smarter. My favourite story about him at that time was of the occasion on which he and his colleagues, finding that Hitler was superstitious and employed an astrologer, acquired one of their own and used him to feed misleading astrological data to Hitler's man, thereby inserting a double dose of irrationality into the decisions of the German High Command. At the time I knew him, Ritchie had been persuaded to allow himself to be elevated to the House of Lords, and he knew just about everyone in British public life. I myself had recruited him some years previously to a kenspeckle bunch of people whom I had assembled with a view to kicking out the incumbents of the Scottish Television franchise. It didn't work, but we had a lot of fun.

At the autumn party I said, 'Ritchie, I've had a good idea.'

'Oh God', he said, 'I hope it costs me less than your last one.' But he said it kindly and I proceeded to explain the plan to buy a cask of Glenfarclas.

He immediately said, 'Great idea. Count me in.' But then added, 'When do you expect to go up to Speyside for your cask?'

When I replied that it wouldn't be immediately he said, 'Make it as soon as you can, would you? I was in Moscow a fortnight ago and I had a heart attack. They tell me I'm likely to have more. If anything happens to me, make sure I get my gallon.'

The end of that year saw some perfectly filthy weather, which continued over Christmas and into the New Year. I had to be careful of the weather, for my route to Speyside took me over some high passes and transport was my old Lagonda (of which more later) which didn't like ice or snow. It was not until the end of January that the forecast seemed promising, and I planned to drive north one Friday morning. I accordingly phoned round my syndicate members early on the Thursday to say that I intended to go the next day, and that the syndicate would meet that evening to divide the spoils. It was late morning when I called Philipstoun House, where Ritchie lived.

The phone was answered by Angus, Ritchie's son, who asked, 'Is that Pip?'

Surprised, I said, 'How did you know it was me?' for I had only said hello.

Angus said, 'Oh, I was expecting your call. It's about the whisky, is it?'

'Yes', I replied. 'Can I speak to your father?'

There was a slight pause, and then he said, 'I'm afraid not. He died an hour ago.'

Another pause and he resumed: 'He called me about nine o'clock and asked me to bring him a dram. A Glenlivet. He sipped it and said, "That's better," for he was in pain. Then he said, "I've a feeling Pip's going to call about that cask of whisky. If I'm gone by then, you must make sure I get my share. You can drink it at my wake."'

We did. Some time later, when a few hundred people gathered to mark Ritchie's passing, we drank a gallon of cask-strength whisky and we were merry as well as sad, which is what a wake is for.

Early on the Friday morning I dressed as though for a trip up the Yukon, for the Lagonda's heater was pitiful. The journey to Glenfarclas and back was uneventful, save for a few spectacular slides (the car wasn't at its best on ice and a hundredweight or so of whisky on its tail didn't improve the roadholding). I took it easy, and by the time I got home that evening the entire syndicate was assembled and evidently in need of comfort – as was I. The first problem was, how to get the cask from car to house – for we lived on the ground floor of a tall tenement and the entry to our door was by way of half a dozen steps and a stone platform. By a bit of muscle and a great deal of goodwill, we wrestled the cask into the lobby and sat it on a stand. We started the bung and, using some plastic pipe, I siphoned some whisky into a jug. I poured drams all round and the syndicate considered the spirit. It was pronounced to be very good, then very good indeed, then definitely as good as I had said it was. As the drams went down the superlatives escalated until, by the third or fourth, I could see that some of the chaps were struggling. (You should remember that at that time almost nobody outwith the industry had experience of whisky at full strength.) So we moved on to the distribution of the spoils. The siphon was employed to fill glass gallon jars, one for each member, and the division turned out to be remarkably accurate. When the pipe would no longer serve, we rolled the cask over and let the last of the whisky drain into a jug. We drank that and the members prepared to depart into the night. Then a difficulty arose: a gallon jar, even a full one, is not a heavy load for a grown man to carry, but when the contents of that jar are precious and the jar is glass, and the carrier has consumed an unknown but certainly substantial amount of whisky, there is cause for a degree of anxiety. I had anticipated that, in what in retrospect appears rather obvious but at the time I was convinced was a stroke of astonishing perspicacity, I ordered a small fleet of taxis. Off the syndicate members went, one by one, each clutching to his breast a gallon of Glenfarclas whisky.

The morning dawned fine and a middling headache was made tolerable by a feeling of relief that the scheme had worked. No calamities, no disasters. Life would return to humdrum normality. And I had a gallon of the best whisky on the planet. It did not occur to me that there might be consequences, other than a very small increase in the sum total of human happiness, which nobody could say was a bad thing. Nor did I realise at first that subsequent events were causally related to what had gone before. I have always been somewhat slow to make such connections, which has allowed me to be more serene about my past than perhaps I ought to be.

The first consequence, of which I slowly became aware, was an increase in the number of visitors to the house. As I have said, I had a lot of pals. From then on, they seemed to drop in more than they had before. Some were quite frank about it. 'We've heard you have some great whisky,' they would say. And of course I would have to invite them in, along with whatever acolytes they had gathered on the way, and give them drams. This naturally led to a diminution in the level of the spirit in my jar, which I was unhappy about, but the iron laws of hospitality must be obeyed and the level kept on going down.

Then the phone calls began. Some were from friends who would say they had heard about the whisky and could they please be included the next time I bought a cask? I would say I had no intention of buying another cask but promised that if I did, I would let them know. Some calls, though, were from perfect strangers. The caller would say, 'You don't know me, but I'm a friend of so-and-so, who is a member of your whisky syndicate. He has just given me some of his whisky and I have to say that I have never tasted anything so fine. Can I join?'

Sometimes, just to get rid of them, I would say, 'Very well. Give me your name and phone number and if I get any more – not that I'm promising anything of the sort – I'll let you know.' And Ritchie's wake didn't help. We had it at the Film House in Edinburgh, of which he had been chairman, so the whisky was exposed to a great many folk whom I didn't know at all, but that didn't seem to stop some of them finding out where the funeral drams had come from.

All of this went on for a few weeks until a new source of grief arose. Members of the syndicate would ring, saying typically: 'I'm running low on whisky. When are you going to fetch some more?' I would reply that I had no intention of doing so, but nobody seemed to believe me, and I was running low myself. Eventually I gave in and called a meeting of the syndicate. All were in need of more whisky. I called them a lot of greedy swine and told them about their friends who wanted to join.

'Fine,' they said, 'let's double the size of the syndicate.'

Their spirit of generosity was no doubt laudable, as was their apparent faith that I could simply magic such stuff out of the air. I reluctantly agreed to ascertain whether the deed could be done again, and at twice the volume.

I called Glenfarclas who said that as far as they were concerned, I had had my cask for this year. And please could they have their empty cask back? After a bit I was able to persuade them to let me have next year's cask and that of the year after. But, they said, no more, for beyond that the whisky would in their opinion be too young.

I should perhaps say a few words of explanation here. Only a few, for if you are reading this it can be assumed that you know the elementary facts of the maturation of spirits in cask. But just in case you don't . . .

Spirits of real quality derive most of their flavour from being matured in cask. Mainly in oak casks, for the chemistry of the *Quercus* genus is such that when it comes in contact with alcohol, many wonderful things happen. When I say 'quality', I mean whisky, brandy and rum mainly, for adventitiously flavoured stuff such as gin or vodka, while pleasant enough, never develops the depth or complexity of fine spirit. When whisky is left in a cask, both the wood and the spirit react, each with the other, over a period of many years. The rate at which these reactions take place depends on many things, of which the condition of the cask prior to filling is probably the most important. The optimum length of maturation for Scotch whisky is generally ten to twelve years, to bring the spirit to perfection of flavour. A very reactive cask may yield a good maturation earlier and a worn-out cask can produce decent whisky after twenty-five or more years. A great many drinkers still cannot be persuaded that older isn't necessarily better, which is no doubt fine for companies holding stocks of old whisky which they would struggle to offload, were real rather than supposed flavour to be the criterion.

Many years ago I happened into a well-known Soho whisky shop one afternoon. Its proprietor, whom for the sake of anonymity we shall call Jack, asked me if I would like to try a dram or two. He produced a couple of perfectly good whiskies and then, with an air of drama, a very dark liquor.

'What do you think of that?' he asked.

I sniffed it once or twice and took a sip.

'Well?' said Jack.

'What is it and how old is it?' I asked.

'It's Springbank,' he replied, 'and it's forty years old.'

I thought for a bit and examined it again. 'I think it was a very good whisky indeed twenty years ago,' I ventured. 'But it's not a good whisky now.'

'I know,' he said, 'but the Japanese can't see beyond the age and they pay me £200 a bottle.'

In fairness I should say that that was a very long time ago

and things have changed a lot since then. Old men in Japan are not alone in being suckers for geriatric spirit and the level of understanding of maturation among Japanese bartenders is now probably the highest in the world. I will come back to the topic of old men and whisky later.

To return to the second syndicate trip: the fates appeared to disapprove, for once again the weather was foul. But the deal had been done and the members were desperate for their drams, so off I set in the old Lagonda. Two casks was a load well beyond the capacity of its admittedly capacious boot, so I borrowed a small trailer. (The vehicle had had a towbar fitted in some previous incarnation, which occasionally offended classic car enthusiasts but was too useful to discard in the interest of mere style.) Off I went, across the Forth to Perth and then up over the Grampians to the headwaters of the Spey and down the A95 to Glenfarclas. The folk at the distillery appeared to be more interested in the car than they were in my buying some of their whisky: I expect if you run a distillery, whisky is common, while very old and classy cars are not.

It was late afternoon, with heavy cloud when I set off for home. After Aviemore the rain started and by the time I had got to the Pass of Drumochter in the Grampian mountains, night had fallen. Now, the combination of rain and darkness was not a circumstance which had figured too prominently in the minds of the vehicle's designers. The headlamps were enormous but the light they gave was yellowish in colour and none too bright. And the windscreen wipers, driven by a Bowden cable from an electric motor, were frankly feeble. So feeble, indeed, that on the dashboard there were two knobs, one for each wiper, which allowed the wiper to be assisted by hand if the going got rough. Believe me, steering in the dark with the right hand while helping the wiper along with the left, is not conducive either to safety or to peace of mind. The knowledge that I had £5000-worth of whisky behind me didn't help either. At least it wasn't snowing.

At some point I pulled into a layby and got out to inspect my load. All was well, save that the trailer lights were not lit. I tried the connections, but with no joy. As things stood, there was little I could do and, since the rear lights of the Lagonda were perfectly visible only a few feet ahead, I considered I was justified in the small infringement of the law implied by carrying on. The journey, otherwise, was uneventful, if long. By the time I got to Edinburgh it was about four o'clock in the morning, but at least the rain had stopped and I began to relax a little. Too soon, I fear, for just as I turned down Craigleith Avenue, I heard the sound of a police patrol car behind me. He overtook and signalled me to pull in. As an officer came up, I wound down the window.

'Yes, officer,' I said. 'What can I do for you?'

The policeman was very civil. 'Would you mind telling me, sir, what is in the barrels on your trailer?'

'I don't mind in the least,' I replied. 'Whisky.'

'Oh,' he said.

There was a pause. Evidently the Lothian constabulary was unaccustomed to people in ancient motor cars transporting whisky in the middle of the night. But I am not a person who would willingly suffer any of his fellow men to experience discomfort, so I said, 'I can assure you that the whisky is perfectly legitimate. It is my property. I have paid the Excise duty on it and the VAT, and I can show you the documents. As far as I am aware, there is no law against a person transporting his own whisky when he pleases.'

This seemed to meet with a grudging acceptance. The second policeman joined us and the situation was explained to him. Neither appeared to be able to think of any law I might be breaking, so I gently explained the nature of my trip. They seemed mollified, but then policeman number one said, 'And are you aware that your trailer lights aren't working?'

'I am,' I said.

Both seemed relieved and one drew a notebook and pencil from his pocket, saying, 'You'll be aware that's an offence?'

'I am,' I said again, 'but before you book me, you might like to hear what I will say to the magistrate. I will tell him how I got out in pitch darkness at the top of the Drumochter Pass to check my load, when I saw that the lights had gone out. I considered leaving five thousand pounds' worth of whisky unattended to keep me within the law, but reckoned that if I did, I would be placing temptation to a greater felony in some poor soul's way.'

'Aye, I see what you mean,' he said, putting his notebook away. 'Where are you going?'

I told him: it was very close.

'Well, we'll just follow you to make sure nobody else stops you.'

I thanked him and, glancing at the casks, he asked forlornly, 'I don't suppose you will be opening one of the casks tonight?'

CHAPTER 3

Some Old Mountaineers

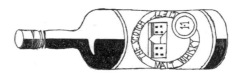

Well, we did open them, a day or so later, with the expanded syndicate, and the members were all well content. The spirit, while slightly different from that of the first cask, was undoubtedly excellent stuff. You should understand that probably none of these people would have described himself as a whisky connoisseur; as far as I know, the species didn't then exist. There were connoisseurs of wine and art and such matters, but not of whisky. For some reason best known to themselves, the Scotch whisky industry didn't encourage the idea of whisky as a potation whose quality was discernible by mere amateurs. Whisky was promoted by inducing consumers to respect a brand and the inducements were for the most part nothing to do with how the stuff tasted. Almost all the whiskies on the market were blends and there was an implication that what blenders did was perfectly opaque to mere mortals, and therefore required no explanation. It was all nonsense, of course. The idea that it might be possible to analyse whisky flavours and describe them for the benefit of consumers simply didn't exist. This may seem incredible to anyone aged fifty or less, but I can assure you that it was the case.

Shortly after the syndicate meeting, the familiar round of enquiries began again and I started to think that I would have to do something for my peace of mind. Two possibilities presented themselves: either I must wind up the syndicate or I must organise it differently. I spent a lot of time with various pals in pubs discussing the matter very seriously – well, maybe not *too* seriously – and it dawned on me that we had struck a seam of pure gold which for some unknown reason had never before been mined. Or if it had, nobody of my acquaintance knew anything about it. So I looked around for advice, and I got it from an unlikely source.

Some time before the first syndicate I had made – I ought really to say renewed – the acquaintance of a man called John Ferguson. Because John plays a seminal part in this story, I ought to describe him. He was a big, genial chap, tall and broad, and what he lacked in hair he more than made up for in muscle. A good guitarist and a better singer of songs, his idea of evening exercise was commonly to swim the Firth of Lorne from Benderloch to Lismore and back, a distance of three miles or so. John was a sociologist by profession and he taught classes in criminology at Strathclyde University and to Scotland's police officers at Tulliallan police college. There was a dark rumour that in his younger days John had got up to a lot of things which made him unusually well-qualified to discourse on criminality, but he kept pretty quiet about it. He was certainly an accomplished poacher, as I can attest, of salmon and deer. (He's dead now, so there can be no harm in telling you this.) And he was a storyteller of genius; and if some of the stories seemed improbable, we made allowances for artistic licence. That said, there was one story, about shooting a stag through a window while lying in his bed in a cottage at the north end of Rannoch Moor, which I discounted, only to have it verified many years after John died.

At the time of the second syndicate I was running my business as an unorthodox tax accountant and had a large and varied clientele, many of them people working as freelances in the arts and in various universities. Penny, my business partner, made an appointment for a chap from Strathclyde University who had got himself into a bit of a tangle with the Inland Revenue and needed help to get out of it. He arrived punctually one morning and we did what was required with due formality. Afterward, as we sat over a cup of coffee, John said, 'Am I right in thinking that you're known as Pip?' for in business I generally went by my full name. 'And when you were young, were you a mountaineer?'

I said, 'Yes, why?'

John hesitated slightly and then said, 'In that case we have met before, and when last you spoke to me, you threatened to kill me.'

Since I have always been the most peaceable of men, it is no exaggeration to say that this came as a surprise. I made sceptical noises and suggested he must be taking me for someone else. John said quite definitely, 'I don't think so.' Then he reminded me.

It was many years before, when we were young and very foolish indeed, on a wet Sunday in Glencoe. (There are few places this side of Kamchatka quite as dismal as Glencoe on a wet Sunday.) Dougal and I were at a loose end and prowling around the glen. We had been to the pub but it was full of hikers, so we got on my motorbike and headed north. We had come all the way from Edinburgh to climb hard rock and that, in the rain, is not an occupation for the faint-hearted. It is very easy to slip on wet rock and a route which in dry conditions would be straightforward, can be a deathtrap in the wet. And worse: there was the possibility that we might attempt a well-known climb and fail. The news would travel and the damage to our reputations as hard men would be great – and nobody would remember that it had been wet. So what to do? We decided to attempt a climb on which generations of mountaineers had invariably failed: a girdle traverse of the north face of Aonach Dubh. While it was dangerous and the chances of success were not great, if we failed we would be in the company of better men than we were.

It's a horrible place. A great, beetling north-facing cliff looming over the valley, vertical for the most part and, where it isn't vertical, overhanging. Now, to a climber, sheer and over-hanging rock present difficulties, but the problems are objective and amenable – or not – to strength, agility and intelligence. But on Aonach Dubh the face consists of loose stones, and the overhangs are mostly grass, and both tend to induce a certain anxiety for they are definitely not susceptible of a rational approach. The one thing to be said for the mountain is that it affords a fine view of the whole valley. I belayed Dougal as he made his way on to the face, which took a while. I was as comfortable as could be expected in the wet and, looking down, saw two climbers making their way up a path below the crag. They waved and I waved back as best I could (the belay was cramped) and hours passed. More hours passed, lots of them, and there came a time when we found ourselves clinging in a shallow groove, belayed to a rock only notionally attached to the mountain, and no obvious way forward or back or up or down. Furthermore, the thing the two of us stood on would have been disdained by a sparrow in search of a landing. It was not a good time and it became worse when we heard a cry from far above, followed by the unmistakable rumble of a rock avalanche. There could be no question: we had to get out of the gully. We did, and cowered under an overhang in a place which our survey of a few minutes earlier had shown incapable of harbouring human life. The rocks roared down the groove and took some of our expensive gear with them.

I don't remember much else that day. We got off the face eventually, but it took us six gruelling hours and into the night. Before darkness fell, the two lads who had caused the trouble reappeared on the path and I am told that in my distress, I yelled at them threats about what would happen, were our paths ever again to cross. That they did not was entirely my fault, for about a fortnight later Nemesis and I had an appointment. The rock this time, though hard, was dry. A bit too hard, perhaps, for I fell about fifty metres and survived thanks to a large juniper bush which, growing on a mountain ledge, broke my fall. Ever since, I have had a tenderness for gin. Arthur, my buddy on that occasion, undoubtedly saved my life that day and went on to have an interesting career. Having being thrown out of Mauritius as an undesirable, he became a harmonica player in Memphis Slim's jazz band in Paris. There aren't a lot of folk from Falkirk who become world-class jazz harmonica players. There is a lot more, but it belongs to another story.

The death threat having been from another life, John and I thereafter formed a close friendship which was to last as long as he did. It revolved around boats and whisky and Scotland's west coast, and a form of joyous, bibulous enterprise known locally as 'high jinks'.

John became a founder member of the syndicate. Since he worked in Glasgow, we would often meet in the Horse Shoe Bar, an old punters' pub in the city centre. One lunchtime, over a beer, I told John of my need for advice about the Scotch whisky industry and he immediately said, 'I know the very man: Russell Sharp.'

Another mountaineer, but active after my time, Russell is a brewer and a scientist, and at the time he was chief chemist at the Chivas Group, ultimately responsible for the quality of some of Scotland's finest whisky. A meeting, also in the Horse Shoe, was arranged. Over bad pies and good beer Russell explained: the quality of our syndicate whisky was down to two things. Firstly, about 80% of the flavour components of any whisky are derived from the maturation in cask, and casks vary hugely. We had been lucky: Glenfarclas had long been buying really fine – and expensive – wood for their maturation. Secondly, we were bottling the whisky at full strength without chill-filtration. The latter is a process whereby the industry ensures that whisky, diluted from its cask strength of around 60% alcohol to the approved 40%, will stay clear of precipitates no matter how cold its storage. This inevitably strips the spirit of some of its flavour.

Russell also explained that if we were thinking about selling such stuff commercially, we could forget it. The Scotch whisky industry had long ago devised means of excluding anyone not of their clan. Were we to use the name of any distillery on a label, we would be liable for a lawsuit for infringement of trade mark, and various other legal impediments. And the people we would be up against were very, very rich and had very, very smart lawyers on their payroll. Having thereby given cause for indigestion, Russell went on to say, 'I think it's a great idea, though, and if you can find a way of doing it, I'd be happy to take part.' That made a big difference. We now had one of the industry's technical experts onside, who would ensure we didn't make any blunders where the quality of our whisky was concerned.

By virtue of his position, Russell was able to tell us something which, while it was no secret, was not prominent in the image which Scotch whisky presented to the public. This was that there was any amount of whisky almost as good and just as distinctive as our casks of Glenfarclas lying about unsold in warehouses because nobody could think of a way of marketing it. And that, if properly approached, distillers and brokers would be more than happy to get it off their hands in return for mere money. He explained to us that because Scotch was sold on the basis of its brand identity, and because what was required of a whisky brand was that every bottle should taste the same, the blender had no use for highly individual casks. The window of our opportunity seemed to be opening.

CHAPTER 4

Leith, The Vaults, Anne Dana

Armed with some knowledge about the whisky, I called a meeting of the syndicate members, told them what I had discovered and suggested that perhaps we should form a company to make the stuff more widely available. I didn't suggest it as a clever wheeze to make a lot of money: as I saw it, here was Scotland's finest, being denied to our fellow Scots by men, many of them foreigners, who *had* made pots of money out of it. It was plainly our duty to rectify a wrong, and if by doing so we should have a lot of fun and drink some uncommonly fine whisky, who could complain about that?

The plan was quite straightforward: we would form ourselves into a private limited company, buy some casks of whisky, bottle their contents and let it be known that it was for sale. If the wildfire which was the news about the syndicate continued to burn, we would have no trouble getting rid of the stuff. I told my prospective investors that there were admittedly obstacles, but I was sure we would find a way of circumventing them. The great majority of the syndicate members were enthusiastic and offered to contribute cash to any such venture.

It was understood that this didn't mean a lot of cash, for we were none of us wealthy. Only a couple demurred, for reasons that only later became apparent. We discussed what the company should be called. I suggested The Scotch Malt Whisky Society, which was agreed *nem com*. My lawyer wasn't so keen when it was put to him. He explained that the Registrar of Companies wouldn't allow any company whose name implied national significance without good reason. The Registrar did in fact enquire why I thought we should have a right to such a grand title. I explained that the prospective shareholders were indeed a Scotch malt whisky society and that, as far as I knew, there was no other. Fair enough, he said, and allowed us the name.

It was the right thing at the right time. Interest in malt whiskies had been growing over the preceding two decades. It was confined mainly to Scotland, though there were outposts beyond the Border. Glenfiddich had led the way with a single-malt bottling but, because it tried to appeal to blended whisky drinkers, it could scarcely be said to carry a banner. Macallan had aroused more interest in the seventies with its policy of sherry-cask maturation, and those who had sampled it needed no convincing as to the benefits of fine-cask maturation. Glenfarclas had long been buying good wood. There were others, but not many, and not all of those of the first water.

There were a number of books about Scotch whisky, but few of them strayed far from the official line, which identified whisky with the rags of the romantic image of Scotland – the Highland glens-tartan-pipers-Harry Lauder portrayal which by then was deservedly in tatters. One book, though, made a difference: David Daiches's *Scotch Whisky, Its Past and Present* which was published in 1969. David, unlike most of the other writers, was a serious scholar with a deep affection for, and understanding of, the country, its history and its people. The book is lyrical without sentimentality and was the first since

Neil Gunn's *Whisky and Scotland*, published in 1935, to look objectively at the practices of the whisky industry.

What really drove malt whiskies in the eighties was a cultural revolution which had been quietly growing in Scotland since the early fifties. It was a process of rediscovery, by the Scots, of a real Scottish identity as opposed to a demeaning, music-hall version in which to be Scottish was to be an object of ridicule. The principal vector of this renaissance was the folksong movement, one of whose leading lights appears a little later in this story. The message was pretty simple: the real Scotland is a lot better than the one you have known until now: you only have to look to find it. Malt whisky – and in particular the full-strength, single-cask version thereof – fitted this narrative to perfection. And it seemed to appeal to the English as much as it did to the Scots.

It was the right thing for quite another reason. The Scotch whisky industry was in recession, with sales falling worldwide, and few of the people who ran the industry had any idea what to do about it. These same people were also sitting on the finest distilled liquor on the entire planet. What an opportunity for us, and how feeble it would be to miss it.

I was to find, moreover, that my discoveries had provided us with a remarkably effective marketing tool. The apparent suppression of the finest whiskies was a great and scandalous story, and when the folk who wrote about such things in the press discovered it, we were to receive the sort of free publicity that well-staffed marketing departments were to hate us for. What is more, it was our story and it just happened to be true. For more than ten years the narrative ran and ran, and it took most of the whisky industry nearly a decade to comprehend what we were doing. No wonder their sales had been declining. And this was Scotland's greatest industry!

At that point we had a product (though with no assurance of supply) and we had the promise of some cash. Obviously we would need some premises for our company. At the time, I thought in terms of a place which we could use as an office, store and maybe bottling line – so it would have to be of a decent size – and, since most of the syndicate lived there, it would have to be in or around Edinburgh. The centre of the town was impracticable, for even then property prices made any such place unattainable. But just down the road was Leith, the old port town which had been physically overtaken by the city's suburban expansion but which remained morally separate. Folk who lived in Leith thought of themselves first as Leithers, though north of the Boundary Bar this was not an identity which carried any implication of elevated social status. Not that Leithers minded much.

Back then it was a very different place. The stones of the tall tenement buildings were dark with many generations of dirt and smoke. Leith Walk, which led from the city down a cobbled mile to the harbour, was a byword for pubs and whores. It is perhaps not to be wondered at that there were few upmarket restaurants in Leith at that time. In fact, there was only one. Skippers had been established in a dark corner close to the old Shetland ferry terminal by my friends Ian and Helen Ruthven. They were pioneering restaurateurs in an era when the expression, in Leith at least, was an oxymoron. They were later to establish the Waterfront Wine Bar, still today one of the town's leading hostelries.

The Waterfront is literally that: it sits on the dockside, in what was once the terminal for the Shetland boat. Ian and I, both of us fond of eels but unable to secure a supply thereof, formed a plan to procure a horse's head which we would lower into the dock. After a day or two, preferably at lunchtime, we would raise the head, alive with eels, which Ian would then cook and offer to his delighted customers. We had no idea where we might find a horse's head minus horse's body, but reasoned that such things must exist, given the existence of horses, which generally had both. Unsurprisingly, Helen vetoed the idea, on the undeniable ground that the customers would probably not be as delighted as we were.

The Water of Leith (not to be confused with the water of Lethe) is a little river which runs through the town to the old harbour and, beyond that, to the docks and the Forth estuary. Beside the pubs and the tenements, the old town consisted of warehouses and whisky bonds. Some of the warehouses were very, very old and a few of them were still handsome. Probably the finest was a four-storey building whose whinstone rubble walls were set behind a high perimeter and a gate. It was called The Vaults, the definite article indicating some pretension to uniqueness. *The* Vaults: not just any old vaults in a port stiff with vaulted chambers. I had long admired it and had no idea what went on behind the wall. One day, thinking this would do very well for what I had in mind, I walked in the gate and climbed the stone stair which runs up the outside wall to first-storey level. A receptionist asked who I was and, in reply to my question, informed me that this was the premises of J. G. Thomson & Co., Scotland's oldest wine merchants. Might I see whoever was in charge, I asked politely. She pressed a button on her desk and presently a middle-aged, balding man in a dark suit appeared. Briefly, I explained my interest in the building and asked whether it might by any chance be possible to buy it? He, equally briefly, answered that by mere coincidence the firm was moving to new premises in a month's time and yes, he was sure that the directors would look favourably on any reasonable offer. I felt the hairs on the back of my neck stiffen, in the way that they do when the zeitgeist seems to be taking command of the ship.

He offered to show me around my prospective purchase. The building does indeed stand on four ancient vaults, which are entered by a stairway from the courtyard. The steps are worn in the middle, in the way that steps wear when trodden for many centuries. Off a dank, dark tunnel run four chambers whose low barrel-ceilings hang with a black fungus brought on wine casks from Bordeaux. Above ground are another four apartments, three of which were lined with stone bays, some still holding wine bottles stacked on their sides. The fourth apartment was a surprise: a white-painted room with two windows between which, set in the wall, is an alcove with a stucco scallop shell above. There is a fireplace and lots of other elaborate plasterwork, evidently old.

On the first floor, up the stairs, were Messrs Thomson's offices, two of which were remarkable. On the left at the stair head, is a handsome room, again with two windows, between which there is a mahogany cabinet whose doors open to disclose a sink with a single tap and racks for holding inverted wine glasses. Evidently a wine-taster's premises. On the right from the little lobby is a chamber equally surprising: a vast room taking up the entire end of the building, the height of its ceiling showing that it also occupies the floor above. There are two fireplaces and many tall windows. It was full of desks and chairs and appeared to be an office. The upper floors of the building were half-empty but harbouring the detritus of many generations of use as a warehouse for wines in bottle and jug.

I was later to discover that there had been a building on the site since at least the fourteenth century. There are few authentic records, but it appears to have been used by the monks of Newbattle Abbey, held in feudal tenure from the superior, the Lord of Restalrig. The monks, or rather their serfs, dug coal from the sour surface of Midlothian and dragged them on sleds to the riverbank below the vaults, where they were dumped to await loading onto ships in return for the wine brought from France. The quayside is still called Coalhill today, though few know why. At some point, probably after the Reformation, the building appears to have fallen into the hands of one of the medieval craft guilds which then controlled commerce: the Vintners' Guild of the Port of Leith. The room with the fancy stucco was where the dean of the guild auctioned cargoes among his members, which is why today it is called the Vintners' Room. John Thomson had bought the building, consisting of a single storey with the vaults beneath, in 1705. In 1785 his descendants had raised it to its present four storeys, using great timber beams brought by sea from Lithuania. The firm was still in existence and it was offering to sell me such a building! If I needed any further incentive, I had it in the fact that the building had been in use in the liquor trade for six or seven hundred years, and that by establishing our business there, we would be carrying on a Scottish tradition – a real one – of great antiquity. Also, it would do nicely for what I had in mind.

I won't go into the detail of the building's restoration. Five of us put up the cash to buy it. One of our members, Ben Tindall, undertook to act as the architect – and an excellent job he made of a horribly difficult project – and I devised a scheme to access government grants to help with the funding. It wasn't a financial success, for the building's fabric turned out to be much more problematic than surveyors had initially predicted. We eventually had to liquidate the company and all five of us lost our money – but by the time that happened the Society was doing well enough to allow us to buy part of the building – the part that mattered most – back from the receiver and we carried on as we were, if somewhat poorer and possibly wiser.

We had just started out on the building project when I advertised for a secretary for my own business, which was suffering from the amount of time I was spending down in Leith. I had found someone for the job, but decided nonetheless to interview another promising applicant. When she arrived I was immediately impressed by her evident perspicacity, her directness of address and her good Scots voice. I explained the situation but said that there was a highly speculative venture in the offing, if she were interested. I outlined the scheme. She *was* interested, and so Anne Dana became our office manager at The Vaults. She would presently become general factotum and then managing director of the company, and would run the entire outfit as the SMWS began its meteoric growth, propelled purely by word of mouth and the excellence of the whisky. The place was a building site and the office of the Society was the present Tasting Room, where Anne and her assistants dealt with members and whisky brokers alike, being charming and efficient despite the holes in the floor and the dust coming up from the building works below.

CHAPTER 5

The Tasting Committee
and Some Pigs' Trotters

When I first had the idea that we might turn our syndicate into a company and allow the great thirsty public to buy our whisky, I tried the idea out on everyone I knew who had any knowledge of the whisky business. The response was usually both enthusiastic and dismissive, 'It's a great idea,' they would say, 'but . . .' After the 'but' would come a good reason why it couldn't be made to work. The most cogent of the reasons was to do with trade mark. I would be told that even if I overcame all the other obstacles, I would be unable to name the distillery where the whisky was made. (Each distillery name had been registered by its owners as trade mark and, were we to use the name, we would be liable for legal action against which we would have no defence.)

It seemed a small thing to impede such a good idea. We had thought of ways round all the other obstacles, so why not this? The answer was simple: no names. I hadn't spent years among the intricacies of linguistic philosophy for nothing – identifying descriptions didn't have to be names. Furthermore, we would give the bottles numbers: the first number on each label would refer to the distillery of origin (and that number would always refer to that distillery) and the next number would identify the individual cask. I reasoned also that for anyone enterprising enough to find our whisky, this would not act as a deterrent. On the contrary, it would add to the feeling of conspiracy which had already begun to develop. Also, if a friend asked a friend what was in the bottle, the Law would be unlikely to crash down on a friend for telling.

We had now reached the point at which the Scotch Malt Whisky Society was in being, but we were feeling our way, for we had little idea of how things would develop. Certainly there was a steady stream of enquiries from people who wanted to know where to get some of that amazingly fine whisky: almost all from friends of syndicate members, or friends of friends of friends ... I was pretty sure that word-of-mouth propagation was the way to go – it *was* – but there seemed no objection to our giving it a helping hand.

Conrad Wilson was a pal, and also an old flame of my business partner, Penny. A journalist, he had a desirable billet for a lover of good food, wine and music, for he was *The Scotsman*'s restaurant, wine and music critic. He was also an enterprising chap who sought to entertain as well as inform his readers and to that end he had formed a wine-tasting circle among his *Scotsman* colleagues. (Not a difficult matter, for they were a hard-drinking lot, like most journos.) The *Scotsman* wine-tasting team ran a piece in the Saturday paper every month, in which, having tasted a dozen or so wines, they gave descriptions of them and awarded each a rating, in points out of a hundred. It wasn't just an excuse to swallow some good grog: they took their duties seriously – maybe *seriously* is the wrong word again – and tasted all the wines blind, collated the scores awarded and averaged them. On the whole they were pretty consistent, which is more than you can say for a lot of folk for whom tasting is their day job.

One evening Conrad took Penny out for dinner and at some point he asked what I was up to. It seems he found the reply of interest and the next morning I got a call. He had heard about The Vaults project and, dimly, about the infant Whisky Society. I asked him down to The Vaults, gave him a hard hat and showed him round. Over a dram, of which he approved, I told him what we were doing. He was intrigued and after the second dram, or perhaps the third, we had arrived at the idea that the *Scotsman* team should come and taste our whiskies – and treat them as they would the wines they normally tasted. As far as I know, this was the first time anyone had seriously suggested inspecting whisky just as if it were a fine wine.

An appointment made, Anne cleared a space in what would become the Members' Room and the first four whiskies were presented in nosing glasses. The tasting team – remember these were Scotsmen who had long experience of their national drink and liked the stuff – were as close to ecstatic as a hardened scribbler could ever expect to be. In their years of inspecting wines, they had never awarded anything more than eighty-three points – a Château Talbot, as I recall – and the big question was, where on their scale of excellence would they locate our whiskies? They ruled out one hundred points, as being an ideal impossible of realisation this side of Paradise. But they gave No. 4, the Highland Park, ninety-nine and the others were very close behind. Conrad wrote the thing up in the Saturday *Scotsman*, and the rest, if not quite history, is at least a bibulous microcosm of it. He described the flavours the team found in the whiskies and, if the terms were unorthodox, at least they established in the public mind two things: that Scotch whiskies could be analysed as you would a wine, and that in terms of quality, there were some which were quite off the wall. The consequence for the Society was an immediate flood of enquiries about membership: most from Lowland

Scotland (for that is where the paper's readership lies) but a surprising number from England and beyond.

I think it was as a result of Conrad's piece that the idea emerged that we might use descriptions of the whiskies as a way of telling our members what we had in bottle. At the time this was a novel idea: most whisky drinkers were the sort of people who thought that wine tasters' vocabulary was strictly for posers. (It's a pity none of us had read George Saintsbury's *Notes on a Cellar Book* by then, or we might have had more confidence.) But the idea of bringing the effete hyperbole of wine to something as self-evidently macho as whisky, now, that was a different matter. I read up on wines and bought all the Sunday papers purely for their wine descriptions. It was obvious that some of the terminology might be imported, but it was also evident that we would have to invent a range of terms, for whiskies display a lot of flavours which are not to be found in most wines. And it would have to be a communal effort, for no one of us was likely to be able to provide anything like an adequate idea of the flavours to be found in whiskies. We decided therefore to have a whisky tasting committee. It soon acquired capital letters: The Tasting Committee. The question was, who should be on it? And what sort of people? And who would choose them? I was quite clear about the last: I would, with the boundless confidence which characterised that time of my life. I was sure that, Russell apart, none of our fellow Board members would be suitable. The Board members, no doubt feeling that there was enough to be doing without any daft new ideas, were inclined to let me get on with it. So I looked about for folk who had experience of drinking whisky and were also handy with words. In the Scotland of 1983 a fair proportion of the population could be said to have met those criteria.

It seemed that most of the descriptions of wines in books or Sunday papers were in the form of similes and metaphors, so I concluded that our tasters should be literate people who would use their knowledge of the language to embroider the poetic on to Russell's prosaic. I therefore invited a few chums to sit at our kitchen table and drink some drams: the sole proviso being that they should talk about them. It was not difficult to find volunteers, for word had got about that there was something going on in Leith to do with whisky.

Besides Russell and me, each at opposite ends of the table, was one of my oldest and dearest friends, Ian Duffield. Ian came originally from Birmingham and could speak Brummagem as well as read Amharic, the ancient language of Ethiopia. He was an historian, bon vivant and a superlative talker who had been a member of the original syndicate. There was Willie Gillies, who at the time was professor of Celtic Studies at Edinburgh University. A poet in both English and Gaelic, Willie would, I was sure, be good for some fine neologisms. I think Bernard Crick was one of us too, but I shall describe him later. And then there was Hamish. Hamish Henderson, a renaissance man if ever there was. Hamish had been a soldier, a scholar and a folklorist. He was himself a poet and the subject of legend and folklore, not in Scotland alone, but in America, Italy and in Germany, to name but a few. He was to be found most evenings in Sandy Bell's bar, his dog Sandy (no relation) beside him and a glass in his hand. His Freedom Come-All-Ye was in a fair way to becoming the anthem of the thinking part of Scotland. If I forget who else was there, it is no disparagement, for in such company few of us would shine.

I had six whiskies for us to taste, with nosing glasses and water to hand. I explained carefully what was wanted: the members of the Committee were firstly to inspect the whisky, nose it without water, with water, and then to taste it. At each stage they were to describe as accurately as possible the flavours they perceived in the spirit. Simile and metaphor were permissible, but only within the confines of strict accuracy. All nodded solemnly and addressed themselves to the first dram.

The solemnity didn't last long. Willie gave what can only be described as a giggle. Now from the learned Professor of Celtic one might reasonably expect many things, but scarcely a giggle. Yet a giggle it undoubtedly was. There were more to come, lots of them, but little in the way of human speech. Russell produced some adjectives which were evidently applicable, and Ian gave of his wit and perception as I had expected. But so far, nothing from Hamish, of whom I had hoped for so much. He sat quietly, his nose in his glass, or just above it, as he savoured the whisky.

'Come on, Hamish,' I said. 'Let's have you. What do you think of it?'

With great reluctance he seemed to tear himself from his reverie. I felt as one would, asking the Buddha to discuss turnips.

'Oh,' he said. 'It's a lovely whisky.' A pause followed, then, 'Chust a lovely whisky.'

That was all we got from him, all blessed evening, save for one occasion on which he ventured: 'It would be a shame to describe such lovely whisky in mere words. Perhaps a pibroch would do.' There was no point in telling him that that was what we were there for.

The first Tasting Committee had to be admitted a failure. I ended up writing the tasting notes myself, based mainly on Russell's remarks. The Committee was subsequently reformed and, if we did not harbour such high hopes, I like to think we produced something of value. Certainly the members of the Society seemed to think so, when we sent them our first newsletter, telling them (in a guarded, roundabout way) what whiskies we had in bottle and appending tasting notes. And, if the labels of whisky bottles around the globe today are any witness, we did something which the entire Scotch whisky industry found worth copying.

We reformed the Tasting Committee from time to time, depending on who was available, and we had some pretty smart guys on it: David Daiches, Derek Cooper and David Mamet spring to mind. (If you don't know who those chaps were, believe me, the fault is yours.) Nobody got paid, all of them did it for the fun of the thing. For many years the two most consistent members were Russell and Ian. For the benefit of readers, I should perhaps say a few words about Ian.

Ian Duffield was one of my closest friends for easily half a century. As is the way of close friends, we drifted in and out of each others' lives, but always came together over a dram sooner or later. I'm not sure I approved entirely of his conduct upon all occasions – and I'm quite sure he can't have approved of mine – but the affection never diminished, certainly not on my side and, I'm pretty sure, on his. That said, I have to deplore his latest exploit, for a fortnight before I wrote this he went and died. You may notice as you read on, that a fair number of the people in this book drop off the perch – it comes, they tell me, of being old. Nothing to do with me. Not that you would have thought age mattered to Ian before the dreaded Alzheimer's got him, for until then age diminished neither his intellect nor his vivacity nor his boisterous wit.

There are some people you take to on first encounter, others whose virtues gradually become apparent. Ian was neither of those: I disliked him on first sight. Perhaps it was a good beginning, for things could only get better. We were very young and while Leslie, to whom I was married, supported us by working as a teacher in a local high school, I was studying German idealist philosophers and employed as a truck driver in the holidays. One day, Leslie said she had met a nice woman called Jill Duffield who was teaching in the same school and lived nearby. Jill had invited her (and presumably me) to a party. They lived in a top flat in Dublin Street in the New Town. Thereabouts the tenements are five or six storeys high and the apartments each enter from a common stairwell which gives out onto the street. Beside the street door is a row of bell pulls, each of which communicates with its owners' flat by means of wires and pulleys.

It was dark when we arrived and I pulled the appropriate bell. We waited. We expected to wait, for in those days there was no communication other than by the bell, and for some reason which I do not recall, I was feeling grumpy. After a bit we heard footsteps on the stair and then the door opened to disclose an extraordinary figure. He was quite tall with red curly hair, red beard and red nose. On his head was a yellow cap the size and shape of an inverted pie bearing some sort of shiny ornament. His entire body was hid from view by a long robe, also yellowish, and also embroidered with braids and tinsels. On his feet were yellow sandals with turned-up toes. He gave us a broad smile with lots of teeth and invited us in. At the time I was bent on being cool, so it is not surprising that I viewed the apparition with disfavour. This was the direct opposite of most that I held dear in the way of personal conduct. As we climbed the long stair, Ian talked continuously. What he said I do not remember but, judging by his chat over the subsequent half-century, it was probably much more amusing than my grumpiness at the time would have conceded.

When we got to the top floor, the party was in full, noisy swing. The other folk at the party seemed much of a piece with our host, if none quite so eccentrically dressed. There were a good many black and brown faces, which in the Edinburgh of the time was unusual, and everyone appeared to be talking at once. This seemed very cheerful and my grumpiness ebbed. I found lots of people willing to talk to me and, though none of them seemed to have the least interest in German idealist philosophy, quite enough were happy to talk about truck driving – or at least to listen to me talking about truck driving – to reconcile me to the company. But it was the buffet which completed my conversion. Ian and Jill had spent the previous few years in Ethiopia and Ian, as a historian, had a professional interest in African history, and an amateur interest in African cooking for he was an accomplished chef, though at the time I did not know it. The spread included lots of dishes which even today would be thought exotic, and, in the centre, a vast platter of pigs' trotters.

One of the respects in which Chinese cuisine differs from that of most other cultures, is in the appreciation of slippery textures. Nobody eats ducks' feet for the solid nutriment they provide, but for the feel as the spicy skin slips off the bones. The consumption of repellent beasts like sea cucumbers can be understood only by such criteria. A boiled pig's trotter has to be appreciated within the same terms of reference. Ditto the humble whelk, which on Scotland's east coast has long been known as a snottery buckie. I expect it is a taste which can be acquired, but for the fortunate few, it is innate. Ian Duffield was one of those; so was I, and on such an unlikely basis was built a firm friendship which lasted for over half a century.

When I first conceived the good idea of buying a cask of whisky, it was to Ian that I broached the scheme. Characteristically, he was all for it. It fitted to perfection his approach to life: grasp it, enjoy it, do your best with what you are given and don't complain about the giver, but seek to circumvent by ingenuity and industry the limitations to which we are all subject. And have a good time while you are about it. In a long career as a teacher in Edinburgh University, Ian inspired a generation of historians who now, scattered around the world, carry on the tradition: people who value what their fellows did in the past and try to ensure that their example is not forgotten. Heaven knows, those who follow us will need it.

As a postscript: I have on my wall a painted cartoon which Ian gave me many years ago. He must have acquired it in Ethiopia. It tells in forty-four frames the story of King Solomon and the Queen of Sheba. Beneath each frame are some squiggly lines which Ian said were Amharic, and which he said he would translate for me one of these days.

'It's the old Biblical story,' he said, 'but with a bit more detail.'

The detail is surprising. Sheba (who of course is black) is received by the great king with much pomp; he then promptly suggests she join him in bed. She declines. Over the next few months he keeps trying and she continues to resist. Then one evening, he gives her a very salty dinner, having first made sure that the only drinking water in the palace is by his bedside. She wakes with a raging thirst and eventually makes her way to the water, whereupon the king grabs her and drags her into bed. The result is eventually Menelek, who becomes the first emperor of Ethiopia.

They didn't teach us about that at my Sunday school, but it's the sort of thing Ian would know about. You can see why his students thought he was a great teacher. I just wish I had got him to do the translation in time, for I don't know anyone else who reads Amharic.

Chapter 6

The Sunday Times, an Albion Van and the RHS

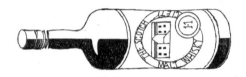

Mainly as a consequence of Conrad's article in the *Scotsman,* we found ourselves with what appeared to be a viable business. Apart from the ongoing saga of The Vaults' restoration, our overheads were not large. So long as Anne and her assistants were prepared to run the show from a building site, we were able to sell our whiskies at prices which, while not cheap, were not enormously in excess of those you might expect to pay in an off-licence. The main components of the retail price were Excise Duty – which, since it was levied on the alcohol content, was high – and Value Added Tax. The latter was a tax levied on a price whose main component was a tax, which seemed iniquitous. It still does. I had a scheme at one point to have the Society campaign for the legalisation of all psychotropic substances on behalf of the nation's whisky drinkers, arguing that if all recreational drugs were taxed as heavily as whisky, the duty on whisky could be reduced, equity served and whisky drinkers made happy. Needless to say, my fellow directors did not think this quite appropriate.

One thing was for sure: we were bottling some very fine whisky. As I mentioned, it was the mid-eighties, the Scotch whisky industry was in one of its periodic doldrums and there was a lot of whisky lying in cask in warehouses, with no immediate prospect of sale. That's not to say that anyone could just go in and buy it. The industry was notoriously clannish and most of the companies were reluctant to sell to anyone they didn't know. And what most of them knew about the Scotch Malt Whisky Society did not make them love us. Sure enough, we never actually named on paper the distillery of origin of any of our spirits, so we could not be accused of infringement of trade mark: but this only made our innovations the more annoying, for there was no obvious way of stopping us save by refusing to sell us whisky. Happily for us, we had two big things in our favour. The first was that the industry then was much less monolithic than it now is, and there were a lot of small firms who paid little attention to the giants. The second was our managing director, Anne Dana, whose charm and cajolery were difficult for macho managements to resist. Also, we were having a lot of fun and getting lots of free publicity in the newspapers.

Having seen the effect of Conrad's article, I began to raise my sights and think about what might be done in the national press. It was apparent that people liked the story of what we were doing almost as much as they liked the whisky. At its core was the notion that some little guys had gone in and, under the noses of one of the country's biggest industries, found a way of bringing to market what was without doubt that industry's finest product. That was a good story: the sort of story whose invention in a big corporation would make a director out of a marketing assistant, though few of the latter seemed to have noticed. Or the former, for that matter. There was more to it, though. I had been reading a lot of Scots history in the preceding few years, and Geoffrey Barrow, who held the

Emeritus Chair in Scotch History at Edinburgh University was a frequent lunchtime companion. Geoffrey pointed out that we were part of a movement which had been growing for the previous few decades. A movement in which Hamish Henderson had been a major influence. Let me explain (briefly, because I have written about this elsewhere, in *Scots on Scotch*).

Scotch whisky was one of the few products which at that time still used the designation 'Scotch', as opposed to 'Scottish'. The reason was that 'Scotch' had, over a century or more, come to be associated with a demeaning, music-hall version of Scottishness which the people of Scotland increasingly came to reject. And my message was – it still is – that the real Scotland is a much better and more serious polity than the ersatz version which is used by advertisers and offered to tourists. It was not difficult to see the link with whisky. Most Scotch whisky is blended whisky and, at the time of which we are speaking, much of the blended whisky was of no great quality. The bottled malts were generally better but they were not many in number and not easily available – and of these, almost all were presented very much like blends, at a strength of 40% alcohol. And all had been chill-filtered, which deprived the spirit of some of its flavour. Nevertheless, popular interest in malts had been growing steadily for the preceding decade, propelled by some enterprising malt distillers and the writings of people like David Daiches and Derek Cooper.

What I did, I suppose, was to bring the two movements together and to present the Scotch Malt Whisky Society as a component in this story. It went down well at tastings, both in Scotland and elsewhere. I was able to tell my audience about many of the icons of Scottishness like the short kilt and the clan tartans which were demonstrably fake – with good historical evidence – and how the real thing was incomparably better and more interesting. Turn then to Scotch whisky and invite people who had been drinking standard blends to inspect a really good malt: it was a gift, an advertiser's dream, a never-failing sales pitch. For, however sceptical the audience might be, it was simplicity itself to demonstrate the truth of my propositions, at least as far as the whisky was concerned.

Armed with this as a sales pitch and with whisky from some really brilliant casks, I looked at the broadsheet press with a view to getting some coverage there. The Sundays would obviously be best, for people spend a lot more time over a Sunday newspaper than they do during the week. Of the Sundays, there was really no question: it had to be *The Sunday Times* – both as regards the socio-economic category of its readership (well-off, middle class) and as regards the personality of its principal wine critic. The latter was Jancis Robinson, the famously acerbic and unapproachable woman who terrorised wine makers throughout Europe and beyond.

I thought, not unreasonably, that the direct approach was likely to be the most successful, and so, having somehow obtained her private telephone number, I called. My reception was polite, but frosty. I reckoned I had about thirty seconds to make my pitch so, without preliminaries, I told her who I was, what I was calling about and why she should listen to me. I do not now recall just what I said, but it must have carried some weight, for I wasn't cut off as I had expected. She asked me for a six-word description of our whisky and I replied that it was the 'best distilled liquor on the planet, bar none'. I was two words over the limit but she seemed taken by my presumption and agreed I might visit her to demonstrate the truth of my proposition. A few days later, I boarded a flight to Heathrow, lugging six bottles of Society whisky and a few nosing glasses. (I was pretty sure I wouldn't need the latter, but no harm in taking precautions.) From the airport I got a taxi up to Belsize Park.

The outcome was an article, with photos, in the *Sunday Times* magazine. It was remarkably complimentary and, given the reputation of the writer, enormously influential. And it produced a flood of requests for membership of the Society which went on for weeks and weeks. If I had to identify one event which raised the Society from a minor curiosity to potentially a serious player, it was this one article. Needless to say, it did not cause the marketing departments of whisky corporations to love either me or the Society.

As I recall, it was getting on for summer by that time, and I had the idea that it would be fun to take Society whiskies to the Royal Highland Show. For those who don't know, the RHS is by far the biggest of all Scotland's great agricultural exhibitions. It happens each June just outside Edinburgh and everyone in the Scottish farming world who wishes to show off their fine beasts goes there. It is the meeting place par excellence for farmers and country folk generally; there is a lot of talk about crops and animals, and a great deal of Scotch whisky is consumed.

My friends up at Denmill had, long before, decided that they would use their knowledge of how farm animals evolved and developed over the centuries, to improve the breed of the indigenous garron – that strong, short-legged, round-bodied creature with a genial disposition. Bred for hard work, a garron can climb with ease a slope that you or I would need to take on hands and knees, which is why it was – and is – greatly favoured by deer stalkers. You can see garrons in Victorian pictures of stalkers and, from a somewhat earlier date, carved on grave slabs with their Pictish riders astride them. That year, Duncan and K had decided to show some of their ponies, in particular a young stallion by the name of McNair. They had come down towing horseboxes and had established themselves in an apartment in the accommodation provided for exhibitors. ('Apartment' is a bit misleading here since the accommodation consisted of rows of wooden shacks which provided facilities for fettling horse gear and, minimally, the necessities of life for the horses' owners. The chalets, as they were inaccurately called, were nevertheless witness to scenes of great conviviality and the consumption of heroic quantities of whisky.)

Time now to introduce Allan Ross. Allan was an old friend who probably described himself in his rare Income Tax returns as a theatre designer. This he undoubtedly was, but in fact Allan was a jack of all trades and master of many, for he was the most omni-competent craftsman I have ever known. (And my friends will tell you that I have enough of certain skills to know a master when I see one.) Allan could turn his hand to almost anything. His architectural drawings would put professionals to shame and his carpentry was as workmanlike as it was exquisite. A year or two previously, Allan had acquired a pile of scrap iron which was all that remained of the Broxburn bread van. The point about this thing was that it had been built by Albion Motors, Scotland's indigenous motor car manufacturer, some time in the 1920s before they went bust. An Albion was the automotive equivalent of the garron. Allan rebuilt the van, which was large, and resurrected its mechanism. The engine was a pile of rust which even when new had been of little distinction, but Allan took it apart and rebuilt it with care and loving kindness. It was a trifle uncertain in its operation, consumed vast quantities of petrol and at its very best would propel the van at about twenty miles per hour. But it did run, and it would move, if slowly. The van, incidentally, was painted dark green.

Having finished the job, Allan had a problem: what would he do with it? It was road-legal, but it was hard to see what anyone might use it for. Vehicles which can do no more than twenty miles per hour were not in great demand, even then. Allan asked if I had any ideas, just as I was contemplating the bibulous habits of exhibitors at the Highland Show, and thinking about how we might recruit them and their friends to the Society. It was another mini-zeitgeist moment and I said, 'Why don't we kit out the van as the outreach arm of The Vaults, and take whisky to sell to the farmers who would join us as soon as they tasted it?'

This we did. Allan fitted out the interior with hardwood panelling as a bar and painted the van (which was already, by chance, in Society green) with our logo. We applied for all the necessary permissions and were granted a temporary liquor licence to dispense whisky. We recruited Society staff and their friends to serve in the bar-van and hand out fliers telling folk about the Society, and on the appointed day I drove the van all the way from Leith to Ingliston, at twenty miles per hour. It was the day before the official opening of the show, traffic was heavy and I was apprehensive lest the thing should break down and cause a major blockage. That Allan was following in his van with a complete tool kit was some consolation. But consolation was not required: we got there and we installed the van, and then I took a couple of bottles round to the shack where I knew Duncan and K would be in residence. They were, and so were a lot of their friends. The friends were receptive to my description of the excellencies of Society whisky and not unwilling to put some to the test. It was like selling steak to the starving.

Life begins early at the RHS, no matter how late the night before may have been, for beasts have to be prepared for judging and, in the case of especially favoured animals, for the show ring itself. While none of us could be said to have been sparky that morning, all were capable and a few of our evening companions called by to express their appreciation of the whisky and their surprise that the resultant hangover was so much milder than they were used to.

The Highland Ponies were inspected early, and McNair was clearly the star of the equine part of the show. I didn't see much of my friends for the next couple of days, for I was too busy telling people about how wonderful our whisky was and

persuading them to try it. The persuasion was none too difficult, though I had to combat the prevailing view that whisky
was just whisky and it was all great, and anyway, who was I
to be telling an Aberdeenshire farmer about it? The trick was
to get them to try: after that it was plain sailing. I don't think
there was one farmer or gamekeeper over the three days of the
show who didn't agree that this was the best thing they had
tasted. A few errant tourists came by and one or two of those
expressed reservations, but they were clearly ignorant peasants
who probably drank raki and liked it.

Toward the end of the second day, when the judging had
been done and the rosettes handed out, I went round to find my
chums delighted that McNair had won a gold, as best-in-class.
It wasn't just the chums who were delighted, McNair seemed
pretty cheery too. And Duncan told me about the final level of
judging which was to take place, in which McNair was to be
entered. The Royal Highland Society awarded a special prize
to the one animal which was judged to be the finest beast in
the entire show. An hour or two later he was as near excited as
I have ever seen Duncan or any Aberdeenshire farmer: McNair
had won the supreme championship and was to be taken on a
victory tour of the main ring of the showground.

Duncan, just in case something might go wrong, had
brought his best kilt and, attired in that and a jersey, he led
McNair into the ring, to cheers and applause from the assembled multitudes. Gravely, holding McNair's bridle, he walked
him round almost the entire ring, eventually stopping in front
of the stand which was inhabited by the judges and the very
important personages of the Royal Highland and Agricultural
Show. The chief judge, Lord Somebody-or-other, made a suitable speech and awarded Duncan a silver cup. Much applause.
He then went over to McNair and pinned the gold rosette on
his bridle, saying something about the most wonderful stallion.
McNair, who knew perfectly well that this was his big moment,

responded magnificently by producing, pink and shining, an erection a yard long. From where I sat, I could see two old ladies at the front of the stand. One nudged the other and gestured. I was unable to hear what was said, but it was plainly to the effect that this chap was the real McCoy.

CHAPTER 7

On Western Seas

The summer came early that year and, in the intoxicating high springtime, John Ferguson and I planned some high jinks in the Western Isles. It was accordingly arranged that he and I would foregather at his cottage in Benderloch. Then, in my boat with some whisky, some food, a small rifle and a quantity of salmon net, we would proceed to the Isles of the Blest. The cottage is in one of the loveliest places imaginable. It lies on the shore of the Firth of Lorne, just opposite the isle of Lismore. In the Gaelic, 'Lismore' means the Great Garden – and indeed it is fertile far beyond any of the surrounding country, for it lies upon a band of limestone which runs right across Scotland from St Cyrus on the east coast all the way to Morvern on the west.

A little ridge of land separates the cottage from the sea, and if you stand on it with your back to Ben Cruachan you can see, beyond Lismore itself, the hills: the Rough Bounds of Morvern and Ardgour in a hundred shades from lilac to deepest imperial purple. To the north are the mounts of Glencoe and away to the south, beyond Kerrera and the entrance to the Sound of

51

Mull, on a clear day loom the cliffs of the Garvellachs, where St Columba's followers (the more ascetic of them) built little beehive cells of loose stones for their dwellings. After more than fifteen hundred years the cells are still in place. So, astonishingly, in Lismore, is the staff of St Moluag. Moluag's was one of the earlier Christian missions to the Picts, a people notoriously resistant to the message of peace and love. (It has to be allowed that Columba was rather more successful than Moluag. When young, Columba had been a successful Irish warlord and I suspect that the Picts knew a hard man when they saw one and his backstory of slaughter carried more weight than did his message of divine goodwill.) Nevertheless, Moluag was ordained bishop for his pains and with the job came a crozier, carved and ornamented with gold leaf. It was still on Lismore, in the care of my friend Deirdre's dad, who rejoiced in the title of the Baron of Bachuil and kept it in a cupboard. I was a little sceptical when first I heard this tale and one day at lunch I asked Geoffrey Barrow, my authority on such things and whom I have already mentioned, 'Is this real? Or is it just another fake Scottish tradition?'

'No, not at all,' he replied. 'It's the real thing. It is one of the more curious byways of Scottish heraldry. The title is held by the hereditary custodian of Moluag's staff and the Livingstones have had the job and the title for about five hundred years. Before that it was Mackays, but the circumstances of the change are a bit vague. As is the question of what it was doing in the years before the Mackays got it.'

There is, about the whole region, a feeling of peace and great antiquity: in good weather that is. When a southerly gale blows, or the midges descend, it's a different matter, and more mundane considerations obtrude.

That Friday afternoon I came down the steps of our Edinburgh house bearing several assorted bags and a case of whisky. As I loaded these into the back of the Lagonda, two women emerged from next door, also bearing bags, though theirs were rucksacks. One of them I recognised: it was Mary, my diminutive neighbour. I was surprised to see her, for Mary, who taught Russian in the university, normally spent her summers in the Soviet archives in Moscow. (At no small danger to herself, as it turned out.) Her companion, whom she introduced, was a tall American. Mary explained that they proposed to tour the Highlands, which neither of them had seen, and that they intended to begin by going to Aviemore. On my enquiring why Aviemore, they replied that they had heard of it and it was in the Highlands. I felt it my duty to tell them just what sort of place Aviemore is, and why they might not like it. Naturally, they asked where else I would suggest. I offered to show them and so they and their sacks got into the car and the three of us rumbled off on the long road to Benderloch. It took five hours and then, in the dark, a stumble round the bay to the cottage, where we found the key beside the door and built a fire of beech logs. My companions passed an agreeable night in the firelit room. The morning was as blissful as only West Highland mornings can be and a white mist hung over Ben Sguliard.

When John arrived, he had a big teenage boy in tow whom he had promised to deliver to a school up by Loch Eil. George, the teenager, was what was used to be known as a natural – not very bright, but very cheerful. John was not in the least surprised to find I had company, for it was a place accustomed to impromptu gatherings. My ladies were delighted to find such unforced hospitality and open to the suggestion that the five of us spend a few days sailing about the Firth. Long afterward, Mary told me that it was when Hecky arrived that they began to wonder whether they had strayed into a fairy tale, or perhaps a pantomime.

Hecky came in a campervan, which he drove straight across the bay, the tide then being out. Hecky was a Glaswegian, small and wiry, his grizzled beard shading into equally grizzled if more scanty hair. And freckles. But first impressions of Hecky tended to focus on his whistle. In his throat, just above his collar, was a small circular aperture lined in silver, through which he whistled. His speech involved both his mouth and his whistle, and after a little practice we found we could understand him. Hecky, John explained, had been diagnosed some years previously with an advanced cancer of the oesophagus. He had submitted to several surgical operations before his doctors discharged him and suggested he prepare for a speedy demise. Hecky wasn't so sure about that and, mixing resignation with optimism, sold all his possessions, bought a campervan and invested the rest of his money in an annuity. The insurance company through which he did this was flustered, for his doctors (who all liked Hecky) were happy to certify him as being but a single step from death's door. It appeared that the actuaries had no experience of a rush job of this kind, so, as a result, Hecky was guaranteed a handsome income for the rest of his days. Of these, he had spent his summers touring Scotland in his campervan, paying calls on his friends – of whom John was one – and occasionally persuading surprisingly respectable women to tolerate his whistle and join him in his van.

We were six happy people sailing on summer seas. We gathered shellfish on the shore: some we ate and some we used for bait, and some we compared with the shells in the midden which the Neolithic inhabitants of Eilean Dubh had left behind them. My boat, the *Gannet*, acquitted herself well; she even occasionally permitted her engine to run, contrary to its inclination, for it was not a lovable machine. And the light winds were variable enough to convey us whither we wished to go, and back again, for the *Gannet* was gaff-rigged and not inclined to sail to windward. We anchored one afternoon off Eilean na Cloiche, where we caught a codling, a saithe and six spotted dogs. I may be wrong about the number of dogfish, for we had been returning them to the sea as reputedly poor eating. John said he recognised the last one we caught as the fellow we had thrown back a few minutes earlier so, in recognition of his persistence, we cut his head off and I cooked him in a tomato sauce. He was perfectly palatable, if ill-matched with the Glenlivet which we were drinking at the time.

After nearly a week of blissful idling, a small cloud hove over the otherwise perfect horizon: we were running short of whisky and George was due up in Loch Eil. The first required a trip to the village to find a phone box from which to call the Society. This I did, and Anne kindly arranged to have a case put on the Oban train for collection in a couple of days. The second was effected rather neatly by Hecky's offering to deliver George to Loch Eil and the ladies, who by that time were expert in Heckyspeak, offering to go along as interpreters.

So one fine morning, the blessed fellowship went their ways. As the campervan bounced from rock to rock across the bay, I readied the *Gannet* for a more serious voyage. She was not a large craft, about thirty feet long, but built of the best Burma teak, probably as a lifeboat for some long-deceased liner. She had been converted to a ketch-rigged cruiser by Dick Morton (of whom more later) before he had been transplanted to Papua New Guinea as the head of the new university's biology department. It is with great affection that I have to say that the conversion left something to be desired, for though Dick was a good geneticist he was a lousy joiner. But he was the most generous of men and one day he rang me up and, having told me about the new job, asked would I like to have the *Gannet*? What was I to do? Tell fate to get lost?

(If you are asking yourself how this story is related to the Scotch Malt Whisky Society, be patient. All of the events of this time, in my life at least, have whisky in them – some at the centre, others at the periphery – and there were few people less peripheral to the Society than John Ferguson and myself.

It was a beautiful relationship, and I only wish it had lasted longer. That it ended wasn't my fault but that of Ferguson, who inconsiderately died.)

We sailed next morning to Oban and tied up to a fishing boat. We collected our whisky from the railway office and we stopped by the *Kylebhan*, a converted trawler, where Kate McKinnon gave us good coffee and even better scones (again, more of Kate later). Whatever my reservations about the effect on Oban of a superfluity of tourists, the wheelhouse of the *Kylebhan* with Kate's scones was a good place to be on a summer morning. So was the Sound of Mull. All day, before a light breeze, we sailed through that broad waterway, with Mull on our left and Morvern on the right. As the long northern evening was drawing in, the breeze obligingly shifted to the south and, unwilling to waste a favourable wind and not enamoured of the engine, we eschewed the delights of Tobermory in favour of a northward turn into Loch na Droma Buidhe: the Loch of the Comely Shoulder, as Willie whimsically translated it.

At the far tip of Morvern, where the Sound of Mull meets Loch Sunart, is a deep bay and athwart the mouth of the bay lies an island whose presence creates a natural harbour, with a narrow entrance at either end navigable only by small boats. Landward access is twenty-seven miles of rough track, which has preserved it from the tourists. Facing the bay is a two-storey keeper's cottage and behind it a stream of clear water falls down the steep. A good place to end a perfect day.

We could smell woodsmoke issuing from the chimney of the house and John, scenting it, said, 'We won't want for supper. Campbell is in residence.' It appeared that Campbell was an old friend of John's: one of the many scattered throughout the Highlands and Lowlands of Scotland. We got the dinghy alongside and, with a bottle of Highland Park in hand, climbed into it. John rowed us ashore where we landed on a patch of perfect turf, or machair as it is known in those parts: good enough to golf on, if anyone could be found to bother with such absurdity in so heavenly a place. In the cottage we found Campbell, his wife Jean, and two friends and numerous children of undisclosed provenance or relationship, but all pleased to see us. The two friends were Oz, a professor of veterinary science at Glasgow University, and his wife. We presented the Highland Park (Conrad's score of ninety-nine, remember) with some confidence that it would be well received. It was. We would of course stay for dinner and, if we wished, thereafter. It appeared that the house was elastic in the matter of beds.

I don't remember much about the rest of the evening, but I do recall with some clarity the events of the following day. I woke early, but not before the children, some of whom were playing in the sun on the machair. It was about seven when I made my way down the narrow stair and found two of the older boys occupied with a motor tricycle – like a big bike but with two wheels at the rear instead of one. It was unwilling to start, so I was able to be of some use, having had some experience of four-stroke motors. We got it going and the boys took turns at vandalising the peace of the morning by roaring around on the thing. At some point one of them asked if I would like to have a go. Nothing loth, I climbed aboard. Though I had never driven a three-wheeler, I had had big bikes when young, so listened with only half an ear to the advice they offered about the machine's handling. Oh, woe. How different my life would have been had I paused for as much as a minute. But no, I roared off, thinking that it had plenty of power but less certain as to its steering. At the end of the track by the bay was a little pier and on to this we went, the trike and I. I tried to turn, as one would on a motorcycle by leaning to one side. This doesn't work on a three-wheeler, and the machine hit a rock, threw me over the wall of the pier, where I hit another rock, hard. Then the machine fell on top of me and all was still. I remember thinking that this was not a good place to be, for the petrol from the tank was dripping down on me. Years before I had had some months of plastic surgery in a hospital ward full of burns cases and I was pretty sure I didn't want to be one myself, so I endeavoured to extract my legs from underneath. This was made problematic by the refusal of my left leg to obey the usual signals. There was also the matter of pain, which made an appearance about then. Not just any old pain, not comparable even to toothache or piles; this was a big pain, big beyond any pain I had experienced in a life in which pains large and little have been fairly common.

I pondered these things for what seemed a long time but was in reality no more than a few minutes. The boys had seen me go over and had run to the house where their parents were by that time getting breakfast. Campbell and Oz arrived at a run and hauled me out. They carried me up and laid me in some long grass, where Campbell attempted to examine my leg. But the pain was by that time so extreme that I shrank from his touch. He asked me what I would like him to do and I said that I just wanted to be left for a while. He said, 'Fine. From what I can see, you'll live, but I wouldn't try to get up if I were you.' If this was brusque, it was consoling, for Campbell was a hotshot orthopaedic surgeon, with practices in Glasgow and Harley Street, and a more authoritative judgement on my leg I would not have found in all the land. Then they all went off for breakfast.

I remember the grass best. It was long grass and a yellowish-green in the bright sunlight. There was a small grasshopper climbing the stem in front of my face. It seemed a pretty good climber but each time it looked like getting to the top, it would lose its grasp and fall back down. It did this every twenty or thirty seconds, as far as I could judge. I then realised that it seemed to be timing its falls by the waves of pain that were flooding through some entity loosely connected with me. There was the big, background pain, whose base note was more-or-less constant. But this would be overlaid at regular intervals by a sharp-pointed pain in a different frequency band altogether. It appeared to the entity that the grasshopper was timing its falls by the acute pains. But how did it know? I contemplated this for a while and was slightly annoyed when the chaps disturbed me by arriving with a makeshift stretcher.

They carried me into the farmhouse and laid me on the stone floor, where Campbell used scissors to cut off my jeans and underwear. This produced such agony (both categories) that I again shrank from his touch and resisted any examination. Some time passed. I persuaded both my pains to park themselves to one side, so my distress was less. Then Oz came in with something in his hand that looked like an oversized syringe. Campbell took it and, very gently, began to prod my groin with a finger. This seemed a strange proceeding in the circumstances so, carefully keeping the pains in their corner, I asked, as reasonably as I could contrive, 'Campbell, will you please tell me what you are doing? And what's that thing Oz brought?'

I think Campbell left his bedside manner behind when he went on holiday, for none of his posh patients would have approved his reply.

'Shut up,' he said. 'I'm looking for your femoral nerve. I used to know where it was when I was a student. And,' he added, in a tone which might or might not have consoled the patients, 'the thing is a hypodermic full of pethidine. It's meant for horses but Oz says it will work fine on you.'

Then there was another, different pain, somewhere high above in a north-easterly direction and then there was peace, for the pethidine had hit the nerve.

Campbell made his examination and a little while later delivered his diagnosis.

'As far as I can see – and we can't be sure without an X-ray

– you have broken your femur. And it looks as though the fracture involves the knee joint.'

This he said was serious and, from my position flat-out on the cold stone floor, I was inclined to agree.

'The femur is the biggest bone in your body,' he went on, 'and mending a fracture in it isn't easy. If you're not to be on crutches for the rest of your life, we have to get you to a big hospital which can do that sort of operation. The problem is how? The pethidine is going to wear off and when it does, the pain is going to come back, possibly worse.'

I discounted the last bit for I reckoned it couldn't be worse. I was wrong.

'Leave it with me,' Campbell said. 'I'll think of something.'

What that something was to be, appeared a little later when Oz came in with a big box marked 'Polyfilla'. Then Campbell arrived with some bed sheets over his shoulder and a bucket. The Polyfilla was mixed with water, the torn-up sheets dunked in it, and within the hour my left leg was encased, from hip to ankle, in rather an elegant plaster cast. They carried me outside and gently lowered me into a deckchair in the sun. Campbell gave me a tumbler and John, who had been back to the boat, produced a bottle of Society Glenfarclas. It was 61% ABV, as I recall.

Campbell said, 'You are going to have to lie there until the plaster is hard enough for you to be moved, which will take all day. The pain will soon be back and we have used up all Oz's supply of pethidine, so I suggest you get stuck into that when it gets too bad. But,' he went on, 'don't overdo it. We can't save your leg if you're dead of alcohol poisoning.'

It is fashionable in medical circles to disparage the anaesthetic power of alcohol. Agreed, it isn't in the same league as morphine or any of its brothers, but it does work if you take the right amount of it. Throughout one of the most perfect West Highland summer days I lay there in the sun, holding both my

pains at bay, having corralled the bigger of the two down by
the stream and the other somewhere out on Loch Sunart, all
courtesy of the good people up at Ballindalloch. The next day
a fishing boat came into the bay – by appointment, as it turned
out – and John carried me in his arms until he was up to his
waist in seawater and laid me gently on the deck. Up Loch
Sunart on glass-calm seas to Salen; in the back of Jean's flower
van (she had a florist's business in Glasgow) over the hills to
Corran; across Loch Linnhe on the ferry, and in the back of
Leslie's Volvo estate to Edinburgh Western General where
Anne, John's wife, who was a senior consultant, was waiting.

I won't go into the grisly sequel, save to say that my left leg
is now held together with what appear on an X-ray to be surprisingly large countersunk-head woodscrews. I expect they are
made of some fancy alloy, of which only a part is iron, for over
the last thirty years airport detectors and I have been in conflict.
At first, when I went through a gate, all the bells would ring.
A few years later, the machines became more discriminating
and all was quiet. Then, after 9/11, they got more sensitive
again. Quieter now, though.

One consequence perhaps worth mentioning: while I was
in hospital and tied to a machine – seemingly out of the San
Gimigniano correction facility for good Christians – they had
controlled the pain with a diamorphine drip, of which I fully
approved. (I didn't like it much when it stopped, though.)
When the hospital discharged me, they gave me a supply of
lesser, but still powerful, analgesics to tide me over the weeks of
physiotherapy which, they stressed, was an integral part of the
treatment. It involved me bending and straightening the knee,
which was painful, while in a variety of improbable positions,
for hours at a time. But it wasn't the pain that got to me in
the end, it was the tedium, and I bethought me of Frances
Gordon's device.

You may recall Frances: she whose party was instrumental in

the formation of my syndicate. When Frances turned seventy, she thought that she was in danger of becoming sluggish both mentally and physically. She dealt with the latter by going on tour: buying a rail ticket from Edinburgh to London and then from London to Paris. From Paris she went by rail – this was in the Soviet seventies – to Moscow and from there to Vladivostok on the Trans-Siberian Railway. She got a boat to Japan and from there to the West Coast of the USA by ship. Across the US by rail, but, failing to find a suitable ship across the Atlantic, Frances flew home. She was tiny, white-haired and evidently vulnerable: she had no trouble of any sort throughout her journey. But it was her technique for overcoming mental decay that interested me. In the course of her journey, Frances had learned by heart all of Shakespeare's sonnets. I emulated her. It made the boredom of physiotherapy tolerable and I was able to save some of the opiates for the boat's medicine chest. I didn't quite capture all of the sonnets and I know that there were many which I did not understand. Still, their perusal is a useful – and everlasting – way of passing the time. If you have to wait for a bus, mentally rehearsing and inspecting a sonnet can make it seem to come quicker. I can still do a few: 'Shall I compare thee to a summer's day . . .'

CHAPTER 8

Champagne, Tobacco and Cannabis

All praise to the people at the Western General, for the femur they fixed has worked perfectly ever since. If anything, it's better than the other one. For a period of some months, though, it somewhat limited my activities and I was able to attend more closely to what was going on at The Vaults. The Society was developing nicely and memberships continued to accrue, simply because people liked to give whisky to their friends and to tell the story. They saw themselves as having done something smart just by finding us, and the publicity from Jancis Robinson's article rumbled on.

By that time we had enough members around the UK for us to go out to meet them, so we began to schedule whisky tastings as a fun and interesting thing to do. We would typically hire a swanky venue and publicise the tasting in our newsletter. When enough members had signed up, a small team of us would take whisky and nosing glasses, and I or another of our people would give a talk about the Society and its whiskies. It wasn't a serious tasting in a professional sense, for nobody was asked to spit out what they had in their mouth. (We found a justification for this in the undeniable existence, when tasting distillate, of a strong aftertaste which happens once you have swallowed and which contributes substantially to the overall experience.) Because of this, and the fact that most of our whiskies had a much higher alcohol content than most people were used to, Society tastings tended to become very jolly affairs and were popular among our members.

At one of our London tastings, I think at the Athenaeum, I was approached by a young journalist who said she wrote for the *Sunday Telegraph*, and would like to do a piece about us. This was obviously to be encouraged, for the *Sunday Telegraph* was in much the same league and demographic spectrum as *The Sunday Times*. We met later and discussed a possible article. Lucy – for that was her name – suggested we might hang it around a visit to some distilleries, which I offered to arrange. While relations with the Scotch whisky industry were in some cases still frosty, enough of them liked us by then for there to be no shortage of distillery owners willing to co-op-erate in return for a mention in the *Sunday Telegraph*. And, in passing, Lucy asked if I would like to accompany her to a tasting of champagnes in London. She explained that this was a tasting of high-quality champagne for professionals, mostly wine critics and buyers. I said I knew almost nothing about champagne, but was happy to give it a try.

The venue was nothing special, but well set-out, with twenty or more very expensive champagnes, flutes and spittoons. The procedure was much as I was accustomed to, save that everyone spat out the wine before going on to the next one. I was intro-duced to a number of the people, most of whom I instantly forgot, but some were big hitters from the wine world whom even I had heard of. We were talking about describing wine with some of the critics when Lucy presented me with a new glass and asked me to nose it and describe its flavours. This seemed a bit unfair, putting me on a spot in which I might easily make an ass of myself. Aware of this, I sniffed the stuff as best I could under the bubbles. Aware also that if I did get it wrong, my credibility would be blown and with it that of the Society, for these guys all wrote for the papers and would be happy to puncture the pretensions of a parvenu. At least I had no doubts as to the description of the flavour: the stuff smelt of biscuits. Not just any old biscuits, but the little vanilla biscuits with a yellow cream sandwich which my mum and her friends ate with tea and which I loathed. So, prepared to be laughed at, I said, 'It smells of biscuits.' I was even able to tell her the brand and the Co-op store she could buy them from. It seems that was the right answer and that most good champagnes smell of biscuits. Not all of the tasters agreed as to my specificity, but I became an OK person as far as that section of the wine trade was concerned. Afterward, over dinner, I said I hoped it had gone well from Lucy's point of view and that I hadn't queered her pitch with the wine trade.

She said, 'On the contrary. They were all terribly impressed.'

Since I had kept fairly quiet, I was unable to see just how I had impressed them.

I mentioned the biscuits but Lucy said, 'Oh no. It was nothing to do with that. They were all terribly impressed by your spitting.'

This took some sorting out, as follows.

As I have mentioned, the tasting room was well-provided with silver buckets which acted as spittoons. All the spittoons were on the floor and I had noticed that the tasters would mostly stand over the bucket and rather dribble into it, which surprised me. I would have expected a confident expectoration from such folk. Thinking little of it, I had spat just as I would usually spit. I explained to Lucy that I came from a society in at least part of which (the male part) spitting was considered a desirable accomplishment. My father had smoked a pipe in which he burnt black twist tobacco, and my grandfather had chewed the stuff. Both of those activities had required frequent expectoration and both my forebears had become very expert. Why not? And though by the time I was a boy the custom of chewing had declined, my dad still smoked his pipe. But the activity was part of the canon of our society and so I too became an adept, though without the tobacco stimulus. At the Dundas Public School I was considered not the best, but a respectable spitter. (Non-Scots should note that the connotation of the phrase 'public school' is quite different north of the Border. My alma mater was high and gaunt and forbidding, and some of its pupils were verging on ragged.)

We agreed that Lucy would come to Scotland and that I would arrange to take her round some of the distilleries she wished to see. The principal of those was Springbank, one of the least accessible of Scotland's many distilleries and, in those days, little visited. Springbank is located in Campbeltown, which lies at the south end of the Mull of Kintyre. As the crow flies, it's not that far from civilisation, for the Mull is a long peninsula which protects the Firth of Clyde from the Atlantic, but at the time of which I write there were no regular connections by sea and, short of hiring a helicopter, you got to Springbank by driving all the way down from Tarbert on Loch Fyne – which itself is scarcely metropolitan – and the roads were all single track, with grass growing down the middle. I phoned the people at Springbank, who were delighted at free publicity in the *Telegraph*, and a date was arranged. Lucy would fly to Glasgow and I would pick her up and take her on to the distillery. Her flight would arrive about 3 p.m. which would allow us time to get clear of the conurbation before stopping for the night, and the next day's run should take us all the way to Campbeltown.

I set out that day – it was a Friday – as usual in the Lagonda, and I set out early (it was always a good idea with the Lagonda to allow time for untoward events). I got to Glasgow about

1 p.m. and, thinking that the airport was only a step away and the Lagonda running fine, considered I might stop at a homely hostelry. There was one I knew well and it was called, with self-conscious absurdity, Babbity Bowster. (Don't ask why. If you are so keen to know, look it up or, better, go there, for it's still there and little changed.) It is part pub and part restaurant, and was the resort of some of my journalist friends, particularly at Friday lunchtimes. As I expected, I found convivial company, though my share of the conviviality had to be restrained on account of my driving. John Linklater was in good form and the chat was flowing nicely when into the group came a tall man dressed with some formality in black jacket and pinstripe. Now the only folk I know in Scotland who wear such garb on a work day are advocates, the Scottish equivalent of barristers, and undertakers. This chap, who was known to all my chums, was called Jock (in Scotland pronounced as you would 'joke') and he had come straight from court where he had been doing his duty by attempting to defend the indefensible.

It appears that some time previously, a fishing boat had been apprehended by the Royal Navy off the coast of Harris. Unable to dump all its cargo in time, when the boarding party arrived they found a little over a ton of cannabis resin. This being as close to red-handed as you can get without dripping blood, the crew were arrested and clapped in irons on board the naval vessel, which escorted the trawler, manned by a naval prize crew, back to Oban and the jail. It was a fine night and the trip was uneventful save that, on entering Oban harbour, the trawler contrived to run aground on the north end of Kerrera, the island which protects Oban from the westerly seas. This was to be the only peg on which Jock could see his way to hang a defence, which he argued as follows.

Kerrera is a long island which runs north and south across the entrance to Oban bay. There is a channel at both north and south ends and *nobody* ever goes aground on Kerrera.

MacBraynes ferries, which are huge, pass through the channel every day. Kerrera is easy to miss; the channel is well-buoyed; the night was fine, the visibility good and even if they had all been in their beds, the boat could probably have found its way to its berth without hitting Kerrera. So how could this be turned into a defence of guys who were without a doubt guilty? Jock took the only possible course, one that was as clear as the entrance to Oban harbour: he cast aspersions upon the veracity of the evidence. With an accomplished use of the disjunctive syllogism, he pointed out that folk have been bringing boats much bigger than our fishing boat into Oban harbour by the northerly entrance for many lifetimes. They have brought them in day or night, winter or summer, drunk or sober and nobody, *nobody* has ever hit Kerrera. So, how could a naval prize crew on a wee fishing boat manage to do it? There were, he said, only two possibilities: either the prize crew, captained by a lieutenant, were totally incompetent, or they had been sampling the cannabis cargo and were all stoned. Clearly the latter was unthinkable, so the former must be true.

He rested his case. It wasn't, he admitted, much of a case, but there wasn't much of a case that could, by any imagination, be made. But the court liked his argument as well as his style and it is possible that, mellowed by amusement, the judge was lenient and Jock had earned his fee. The only people who weren't amused were the Navy. Jock's clients were sent down for a few years and justice, in its way, was served.

When I picked Lucy up from Glasgow airport she was a bit surprised by the transport, but I had brought lots of rugs as well as the travelling bearskin, so she wouldn't be cold. We stayed somewhere on Loch Lomondside that night and in the morning made the long drive down to Campbeltown. The people at Springbank could not have been more welcoming and were delighted to show us some of their treasures. The latter were in sherry butts or puncheons – the latter a huge, round-bellied cask – and many of them had lain undisturbed in their damp warehouse for a generation or more. Tasting their contents was no problem and the leviathans were rolled out, their bungs started and samples drawn. The quality of the whisky was just staggering, yet as the Scotch whisky industry then marketed its products, there was no machinery for selling such stuff, for there did not exist in the public mind the idea that it existed. And Springbank didn't have the people or the money to create such a perception, so were delighted that they might get a mention in a high Tory paper like the *Sunday Telegraph*.

The following day was wet: West Coast wet, which is very wet indeed. As we drove up the narrow road (where there was, to my relief, little traffic) I introduced Lucy to the operation of the windscreen wipers. I drove while she turned the knob which helped the wiper-motor do its job, occasionally passing me the rag I used to clear the mist from the inside of the screen. Things were not rosy and, after an hour or two, we were both in need of some coffee and comfort. In that era there was little chance of either for, north of the Central Belt, Scotland was a culinary desert, the spacing of whose oases would have been thought a disgrace in the Sahara. Besides, Tarbert was shut. It was, after all, Sunday, so this was to be expected, but enquiries at the hotel disclosed that there had been a big bash the night before and the entire population was in its bed. So, no coffee. At least we had plenty diesel, so we continued north, I assuring Lucy without conviction that we would inevitably find something to drink at Lochgilphead or Kilmelford or, surely, Oban itself.

You may have guessed: none of the villages on the road were productive of coffee. Some claimed to have such a potation but close inspection disclosed different varieties of ersatz. That left Oban as our best chance. Lucy, who had never been in

Oban before, asked about its coffee houses and mere honesty constrained me to admit that things were little different there. My one hope was that the *Kylebhan* might be in harbour, it being a Sunday. If it were, I could promise comestibles and conversation to please the most discerning. It was. We drove down to the fish pier and there, nestling beyond a couple of seine netters, was the *Kylebhan*: scruffy but businesslike, with a big wheelhouse and a stack of diving bottles. There was, however, the small matter of getting there. Or, more precisely, getting Lucy there, for the tide was out and it was a long way down the slippery, weed-hung ladder.

I immobilised the car as best I could (it had no door locks) and pointed out the *Kylebhan*. Lucy looked at the boat and then at the quayside ladder.

'You mean I have to climb down there?' she asked, incredulity striving with improbability.

'Yes,' I said. 'It's easier than it looks. If you like, I will go down first and catch you if you slip.'

I had as much chance of stopping a hundredweight of coal as I did of arresting a falling *Sunday Telegraph* wine critic, but she seemed reassured and I lowered myself onto the ladder. This met with approval from three fishermen who had been shelling scallops and watched appreciatively as Lucy lowered her bottom over the edge of the quay.

She got a round of applause when she reached the deck and helping hands to get her from one boat to the next. Somebody hailed the *Kylebhan* and Kate put her head out of the wheelhouse door.

'Where have you been?' she asked. 'We were expecting you ages ago. The coffee is on the hob and the scones are due out of the oven, so your timing is good. Cubby is down in the engine room somewhere,' she said, referring to her husband who was skipper, pilot, navigator and engineer of the ship.

Cubby was a MacKinnon; one of the Canna MacKinnons

and as such licensed by the Board of Trade to convey passengers and cargo anywhere between the Mull of Kintyre and
Cape Wrath, despite a complete absence of formal qualifica-
tions. He did, however, know every reef and tide-race, every
buoy and wreck on hundreds of miles of ferocious coast. And,
more important even than the Board of Trade (who were of less
consequence than the United Nations, but only just) were the
insurers, who deemed Cubby a good risk. So did the National
Trust for Scotland, an organisation which entrusted Cubby
with the conveyance of its squads of volunteers and visitors to
and from the distant isles of St Kilda every summer.

Some banging noises indicated that something was afoot
and presently an oily figure in a boiler suit appeared from under
a hatch cover. I made the introduction. I could see at once that
Cubby was much taken with Lucy and she delighted with him.
Kate just looked on benevolently.

'The old bugger charms them all, doesn't he?' she said to me
in an aside. 'But there's no harm in him.'

A little less benevolently she added, 'There better not be.'

I find that in life very few things quite live up to our expec-
tations, but Kate's coffee was one which exceeded them. It was
black and strong and very, very good – and matched only by
the excellence of her scones which she produced, golden brown
from the oven and soon slathered with butter. Lucy, who was a
person of strong appetites, gobbled several, muttering between
mouthfuls something apologetic about heart attacks.

'Nobody dies of heart attacks hereabouts,' Kate said. 'Drink,
yes, but not heart attacks.' This while producing a bottle of
whisky, for the hospitality of the ship required it even though
it was still morning.

Late morning, that is, and nearly lunchtime. As soon as we
looked as though we might eat anything more, Kate produced
lunch. After it, more whisky and the news of what had been
happening in the world since I was last there. ('The world' in

this case being the coast from Cape Wrath to the Mull, with associated landward parts, but not a lot else.) I naturally told my story of the Glasgow court case and the apprehension of the drug smugglers. Cubby of course knew all about it and was able to add a deal of detail to my outline. I asked what he thought of the case for the defence. Cubby threw his head back and roared with laughter.

'Och yes,' he said in his soft West Highland accent. 'We always used to say that there were three things that were no use at all on a boat. They were a lawnmower, a top hat and a Royal Navy Officer.'

CHAPTER 9

Dalnamain

Early in this sad tale I described my chum John Ferguson, an old mountaineer and a man who was up for high jinks of all sorts. John was a member of a club of Glasgow climbers called the Creag Dhu who regarded themselves – with justification – as the hard men of Scottish mountaineering. Climbing mountains had been the prerogative of gentlemen amateurs from the beginning: only people of means and leisure could afford to spend their time in such pursuits. But in the 1930s a bunch of unemployed guys from Glasgow had taken to spending their enforced leisure in the hills instead of on the grimy streets of Glasgow. Being in the hills, and seeing gentlemen climbers, they not unnaturally thought they might do likewise. They did, and because they didn't have the books which told them which things were climbable and which were not, they sported on crags which were deemed impossible by the respectable members of the Scottish Mountaineering Club.

The thirties were hungry days in the west of Scotland, and in the course of their wanderings the Dhu saw a great deal of good grub on the hills and in the rivers. This took the form mainly of venison and salmon, and the Dhu became expert in procuring both, for themselves and their friends, without coming to the notice of the keepers employed by the owners of the Highland estates. So was a tradition born, and membership of the Creag Dhu often involved poaching as much as (and sometimes at the same time as) mountaineering. It should be noted that these chaps were not commercial poachers: they did it to feed their friends and families. On the other hand, they would have been less than human if they had not taken a pride in what they did, and in doing it well. By the late fifties, when I first knew them, it had become more in the nature of a club tradition than a serious pursuit.

I should perhaps explain the attitude of the Scottish people to poaching game. A tiny number of (mostly rich, sometimes very rich) people own most of the Highlands. This they do not for the profit such ownership brings, for Highland land rarely yields a surplus and normally requires a hefty cash subvention. Some own land because that is what they suppose that the sort of people they are – or would like to be – ought to do. Others do it so they can kill things as a leisure pursuit. Some do it merely so that they can look at large tracts of moorland and take pleasure in the thought that they own it. For almost all these people, part of the pleasure in owning land is to keep other people out of it. And for the people who like blood sports, of making sure nobody but they and their friends get to kill anything. This doesn't go down too well with a large part of the general population who, having a set of attitudes which derive from a Celtic past in which all land was communally owned, have long taken the view that they have a right to roam where they please. And some of them think they should have a corresponding right to kill wild things to eat them. One can see where the Creag Dhu were coming from and how their actions emerged from a moral landscape different from that of alien landowners. (The Scottish government have now changed the rules about who may go where – but not about knocking off the fauna, which is understandable.)

It doesn't take a lot of imagination to see how the Creag Dhu went down with the SMC, many of whose early members were aristocrats who took a very dim view indeed of poachers. Not only were these folk stealing their fish, they were climbing their mountains too, and climbing impossible ones at that. An animosity grew up which did not approach a resolution until, in the late fifties, a hard-climbing crew emerged in Edinburgh who would challenge the Dhu on their own ground – of climbing though, not of poaching. The leading lights of this group were Robin Smith and Dougal Haston. Smith, alas, died young in the Pamirs, but Haston went on to climb the north face of Everest, surely the greatest mountaineering route on the planet. Smith gave the greater offence, though, by climbing a horrible (and horribly dangerous) route on the appropriately named Slime Wall of Buachaille Etive Mor, which the Dhu regarded as their domestic patch. And he had the cheek to name it 'Shibboleth'. Not all of the Dhu got the joke, but those who did were none too pleased. I was a very minor member of the Edinburgh group, so saw the rivalry at close quarters.

Just as the Dhu looked down on the SMC for being middle-class, so we took the battle to the enemy (i.e. friends) by implying that they couldn't be serious climbers if they spent a lot of their time poaching. It all came to a head one night in the public bar of the Café Royal, in Edinburgh (which wasn't then nearly as posh as it sounds). One of our lads, Andy, who had recently got married, said, 'Anyway, why go to the trouble of creeping about in the dark and wet, when in this very pub you can buy a fish [which invariably meant a salmon] for a tenner or so?'

This was a powerful argument and the Dhus protested, 'How big a fish?'

'Fourteen pounds,' Andy replied. 'I got it from a chap at the back door last night.'

A chorus of incredulity from the Dhu.

'And,' he went on, 'if you don't believe me you can come and eat it, for Mary is cooking it as we speak.'

Beer in bottle was bought and out the crew sallied. Andy had a good job and therefore a dining table, around which all congregated. No starters, no soup or any of that nonsense, only the main course. We had time for a few more beers before Andy proudly came through the door bearing a long dish covered with a cloth. He laid it on the table and, saying 'There,' he proudly removed the cloth to disclose a rather splendid codfish. We all enjoyed the cod (to my mind a better fish than salmon anyway), but Andy's reputation was in tatters.

Though John played an important part in the genesis of the Society, he had little interest in business, and while he became a director of the company, he was more likely to be found in a pub or his cottage in Benderloch, singing songs, than in The Vaults. He contracted a cancer which eventually killed him despite the best efforts of Campbell (whom I have mentioned) and his colleagues. But until then we had some great times, and John would occasionally demonstrate his skills in the matter of stags and salmon. Indeed, we even went so far as to plan the establishment of an enterprise which would put those skills to good use. It was part of our overarching intention of presenting to the public the true face of the real Scotland, though I have to admit that the occupation of the moral high ground did not figure quite so prominently as it did with the Society.

We were moved in part by our loathing for the tourist trade and the trash and trumpery which was what it mostly offered to visitors. (If you don't know what I'm talking about here, take a look at the desecration of Edinburgh's Royal Mile.) Our plan was to offer a unique experience to a small number of paying guests. We were to establish a company to be called Filthy Highland Holidays. Originally the idea was to show visitors what Scotland was really like: rain, cold, midges, bad food, bad drink, damp beds and so on, all of which could be guaranteed. There would even be a place for the tartan dollies. But on consideration we could see that this programme, however authentic, might meet with customer resistance, and so we took another tack.

The new plan was to utilise the skills, mostly now dormant, of the Hyde side of the Creag Dhu, mainly in the person of John. It had its origin in a magazine which had come into my hands. This publication stemmed from the USA but was clearly aimed at an international readership of gun enthusiasts: hunters, or people who would like to be hunters, of wild game. It was evident from the magazine that there were a great many such folk and that a lot of them were prepared to spend very large amounts of money in pursuit of their obsession. After reading the magazine John pointed out something I hadn't noticed. This was that the armaments on offer were such that the average ten-year-old could face a raging bull elephant with a very good chance of killing it from half a mile away, and that this made the whole thing a bit boring.

John suggested, 'Why don't we offer them something really difficult? Like poaching. Any fool can kill a deer or a salmon if he has the right gear, but to do it at night, under the eyes of a ghillie, now that takes a bit of skill.'

So was born another good idea. Over the next few weeks (and over a great many drams) the plan took shape. We would spread the word with the greatest subtlety. Like the Society, there would be no paid adverts. We first had to identify a Highland sporting estate which had fallen on hard times, but possessed a fine shooting lodge. We would renovate and furnish the lodge to be far more luxurious than its Victorian owners could have imagined and we would staff it with a cordon bleu chef and a company of cheerful hookers. Society whiskies would of course be on offer, as well as first-rate wines.

The estate itself would not be hunted or fished, save during the day for training purposes. But at night we would poach the neighbouring estates and the aim would be to enable our guests to take fish from the river and beast from the hill without the knowledge of the estate's owners.

This would be a High Jink if ever there was one. (John Buchan had suggested something similar in his novel *John Macnab*, but without the hookers.) The owners of the adjoining territories would have to be in on the plan, but in the greatest secrecy and for a cut of the profits. The police would have to know, too, and donations would have to be made to the Bobbies' Benevolent Fund or whatever. Our rich shooters would be guaranteed to be cold, wet, midge-bitten and possibly (if caught) thrown into the police cells. But nobody would be held for more than a few hours and nobody would actually be charged. And the hunters, even those who had been arrested (*especially* those who had been arrested) would have a story to tell their friends for ever after. And we would all make lots of money and have a lot of fun. We couldn't see how it could fail. Alas, it depended on John and, as I have said, he inconveniently died.

For many years I had a little cottage high in a valley in the eastern Highlands, in Sutherland, to which I would retreat when life became too burdensome. (It may seem odd that a county in the far north should be called Sutherland, or 'land of the south', but about a thousand years ago it got its name from the Vikings, who came from even further north.) I rented the cottage from an estate which owned a lot of the land round about and there I would go, summer or winter, and repair my shredded sanity. It was a saintly place of great, if chilly, serenity. To get to it you took the road north from Inverness for a couple of hours, then, leaving the main road, a single-track road which, threading through a swamp and an alder forest, soon rose into the hills, at which point, high on a hillside, the cottage would come into view. It was an old keeper's or shepherd's cottage and evidently of some antiquity. Certainly the place has been inhabited for hundreds, perhaps thousands of years.

There is a chambered cairn twenty yards from the back door and a tumulus at the foot of the hill with a depression in one end which grave robbers, probably Vikings, left when they plundered it a millennium ago. In the valley is a small field of good grass with, in the middle, a standing stone. I think the marks on one of the corners of the stone are ogham but, since nobody can read Pictish ogham now, it's a bit academic.

In winter the place can be truly magical. To the south on the horizon are seven hills over which, on a clear night, the stars of Orion's Belt rise, blazing. It is, though, a cold place to arrive at midnight, after six or seven hours' driving. The lighting is by candle and oil lamp, though there is a generator which will, if cajoled, provide electricity. The generator is powered by a twin-cylinder Lister diesel which does not like cold weather. No diesels like cold weather, but this one is particularly difficult. It's not surprising, really. A diesel engine works by compressing oil and air to the point at which they ignite spontaneously. Midnight on a freezing hillside is not conducive to spontaneity in a diesel. One winter evening I arrived and, for some reason, I needed electric light – I forget why. No amount of cranking would elicit even a cough from the Lister. I had of course brought some whisky and I thought of a consolatory dram when, in a flash which would have been familiar to Leonardo, I saw the solution. I uncorked the Highland Park and poured a libation into the Lister's air filter. Then I produced a matchbox and struck a light. This I applied to the whisky in the air filter, which blazed with a blue flame. I decompressed the cylinders and turned the handle, sucking burning whisky into the engine. After the third turn, it fired. I have used the technique many times since and can recommend it without reservation.

A little river flows through the valley from the loch at its head to the sea, a distance of about seven or eight miles. Buzzards hunt in the alder wood and once, standing in the phone box at the bottom of the road, I watched an osprey flash over the sea and lift a fish in its claws. The river is lovely. It is a small river, but in every respect all that a river ought to be: its water brown from the peat in the hills but perfectly clear, and in the pools you can see trout and, sometimes, a salmon.

John would occasionally join me in my trips to the cottage and I often saw him eyeing the river.

'Do you realise,' he once said offhandedly, 'you have one of the best poaching rivers I have ever seen? I could lift a fish from that river and scarcely get my hands wet.'

I had long ago told him that the river was off-limits. I had no intention of endangering my tenancy by taking the estate's salmon, and I was on good terms with the owner who had always been more than fair to me. Also, I knew about the river and its poaching possibilities, and I thought I would bide my time. I pointed out to John the little jeep which the keeper drove up the glen every morning as a warning to would-be poachers, but John dismissed this as being beneath the notice of an expert such as he.

In a little farm just over the hill I had a friend called Alec. The farm had an unusual name and so did Alec, who was a Stuart. I asked him about it once, for this was a land of Mackays and Mackenzies, and a Stuart was evidently an incomer. Alec confirmed it: his family had indeed been incomers – in the early seventeenth century. Alec would sometimes ask me over for a dram and once when he did so, John was staying, so went with me. There was then a meeting I had hoped might happen, for there was another guest, the road mender, Jock by name. The two might have been brothers, so little did they seem to need to say to each other for a perfect understanding, and the story came out as naturally as a snowdrop in the spring.

Jock was in charge of a road-mending gang. There were four or five of them besides himself. They had a little lorry on which, of a morning, using the lorry's hydraulic crane they would load some picks and shovels, a little compressor and a pneumatic drill, a small self-powered roller and a quantity of smoking bituminous gravel. Jock was the gaffer for the district and it was his decision as to which bit of road most needed mending. If I tell you that the road up our valley had grass growing down the middle (like so many roads in this book), it will be apparent that traffic was not so heavy as to necessitate frequent repair.

Jock was on good terms with the keeper, who would some-times stop on his way up the valley to chat, and perhaps take a mug of tea. The keeper was young and keen, and not the sharpest, else he might have made a connection between the weather and the road repairs. Perhaps that's unfair, for there was a delay between the onset of heavy rain and the appearance of the road-mending gang, so that it was not apparent that the one might be said to be causally related to the other. This is how it happened.

Within eight hours or so of a period of heavy rain, the river would rise and the salmon would run from the sea to the loch at the top of the valley. After a wet night, Jock would decide that our road needed mending so quite early in the morning the squad would drive up the valley. They would stop at the most ragged bit of road (there were plenty to choose from) and they would set up traffic lights to control the half-dozen vehicles which might be expected to use the road that day. Then they would unload all their gear and they would dig up a stretch of road. By lunchtime the piece of road would be dug and if a car came along it would be carefully shepherded past the rough patch. The menders would take their dinner boxes and, if the day were fine, they would sit by the roadside and eat their dinners for the hour to which they were by law entitled.

At some point Jock would slip down to the river, which was at no point more than a few minutes' walk from the road. Using a gaff or similar implement he would abstract a salmon or two from the pool, wrap them in a hessian sack and put them in the back of the cabin of the truck. This would generally take only a few minutes, for he was a professional. In the afternoon, the chaps would spread bitumen and gravel on the road and then they would roll it with the little roller; they would dismantle the traffic lights and they would pack all the gear into the truck and by four o'clock they would depart. I have been with John Ferguson in the company of the good and the great, and I have rarely seen him look on anyone with such frank admiration.

*

While I am on the subject of our valley, I hope I may be forgiven for telling you about Alec and the life insurance. Alec was a sheep farmer. His own farm had a fair bit of arable and a lot of hill on which, in the warmer months, he ran sheep. The people who owned our valley, in order to reduce their overheads, let the grazing in the valley to Alec so that, besides his own land, he had some nine miles of rough country on which to graze his sheep. This didn't mean a vast number of animals though, for Alec was a responsible and kindly man who would not overstock the land. But it did mean he had to spend some time looking after the sheep. He would call in at the cottage if I were in residence and would take a cup of tea in the morning; a dram in the afternoon.

Late one heavy summer day Alec called by. It was evident from the way he handled his glass that he had something on his mind. We talked about the weather, which wasn't much of a subject for the weather that year had been in no way unusual. Then, to my surprise, he asked what I thought about life insurance. If he had asked my opinion of netsuke I could not have been more astonished. Now I knew little about life insurance, always having been improvident in such things, but I was perfectly happy to talk about it, for I sensed that something lay beneath. It seemed that Alec's wife had been agitating for him to take out life insurance and he was worried. As tactfully as I could, I asked about their personal relations, for when a wife becomes interested in life insurance it is always prudent to consider the possibility of assassination.

But it seemed they were on the best of terms. The trouble had stemmed from an insurance salesman who had come calling and had shown the wife some astonishing calculations which implied vast riches in the future for very modest contributions in the present. I couldn't contribute much to this debate and Alec left me curious as to how it would pan out. It was to be more than a year before I found out.

Alec had allowed himself to be persuaded and the insurance man had come back to present his projections, none of which Alec believed, but for the sake of domestic peace he agreed to take out a policy. The man helped them fill in all the forms and then asked Alec, who was then aged about forty-five, the name of his doctor. This presented a difficulty.

'I don't have a doctor,' Alec said. The insurance man failed to understand.

'Which local practice are you registered with?' he asked. 'Who do you call when you are ill?'

'I don't get ill,' Alec replied.

It took some time for the insurance man to digest this. Not only did Alec not get ill, he had never been ill and had never been registered with any medical practice.

'Well,' the insurance man said, 'I'm afraid I will have to ask you to register with a local practice and ask for a medical examination, for we need a medical certificate to support the application for life insurance.'

So Alec was registered and duly examined. When he had finished the examination the young doctor said, 'You're pretty fit for your age. What do you do?'

Alec said, 'I'm a sheep farmer.'

'Do you take a lot of exercise?' the doctor, a chiel from Glasgow, asked.

'Depends on what you mean by exercise,' Alec replied.

The doctor, apparently not the quickest on the draw, came back: 'Do you play any sport? Or go jogging?'

(Jogging, a slow, laborious form of running for fat people was then in vogue.)

'No,' Alec replied. 'I don't think I would have the energy.'

The doctor evidently felt by this time that he was on safe ground and persisted, 'Would you like to tell me just what you did today, so that I can get an idea of your level of activity?'

'Well,' Alec replied, 'in the morning, early, I went up the glen after a wheen of yowes and I brought them down by dinnertime. But in the afternoon I thought to myself that I had probably missed some, so I went up again and, sure enough, there were half a dozen more. So I brought them down too. That's about all. And I don't feel much like going jogging.'

Happily the doctor had begun to grasp the mettle of the man, for he asked for more particulars, which were as follows. The glen, from Alec's farm to the head, is about nine miles as the crow flies and it is very rough ground in places. Alec had covered about thirty-six miles that day, the equivalent of easily fifty on a road. The doctor, thus apprised, looked at him with astonishment and, without ado, signed the medical certificate.

Chapter 10

The Stove and the Indians

It should be the other way round, really, but it reads better that way. The Indians came before the stove exploded and the two are only indirectly related, in that both involve whisky and my continuing existence in this vale of crocodile tears. I suppose that is less than clear. Let me explain.

The more successful the Society became, the greater our need for casks of fine, mature whisky, and the more dependent we were on the goodwill of the people who owned the stocks of the same. We were very careful to avoid giving offence and Anne continued her cajoling of the industry, as did I, if in a different way. Nonetheless, we were always on the lookout for fine casks and at that time they could be found in some unlikely places. What we didn't know – what almost nobody knew – was that in a warehouse not ten miles away lay one of the greatest stocks of fine malts in existence. And in a place where nobody – certainly not we – would have thought to look.

Drambuie will, I should think, be known to everyone who is remotely interested in Scotch whisky. It is the original whisky liqueur and a bottle is to be found on the gantry of every self-respecting bar in the world. Nobody drinks a lot of it, but millions of people occasionally drink a little and its worldwide sales are enormous. It is made from quality Scotch whisky and honey, and various other ingredients; the latter a closely guarded secret. At the time of which I write, the company was owned by the MacKinnon family which consisted of Mrs MacKinnon and her two sons. The base of its operations was in Broxburn, to the west of Edinburgh, where the blending of the liqueur took place. The description of this process reads like a blurb from an advertisement or a tourist brochure but, as I was to discover, was actually true. After the staff had mixed the principal ingredients for each batch of the liqueur, Mrs MacKinnon would retire to an upstairs laboratory where she would concoct the elixir which, added to the vat, would make it into Drambuie.

The MacKinnons had owned the business since its inception, which was a very long time ago. The story goes that the secret was divulged to an ancestor by none other than Prince Charles Edward Stuart, in the course of his flight after Culloden. Whether this is true or not, I do not presume to judge, though the likelihood of a Stuart prince of the blood being concerned with a recipe for liqueur seems pretty small, as does the probability of his pausing long enough to tell folks about it, given that the redcoats were hot on his trail and he would die a nasty death if caught. It's a good story, though, and we should have fellow-feeling with all who use such things to sell Scotch drink.

The family had managed the business since its inception but, as is the way with such things, there came a time when its heirs thought that running a liquor company might not be what they wanted to do with their lives. So they looked around for someone who would manage the business. He would have to be a person of exceptional talent who understood both the pressures of running a family-owned firm and the corporate environment in which the company would operate. They were fortunate in finding Peter Darbyshire who had all those talents and a great many more.

On coming to the job of managing director, Peter made a review of the whole business and I expect he was surprised by what he found. In the warehouse in Broxburn was an incredible stock of maturing malts, all in first-class casks, for the company had long been able to afford the best. And in addition, there were stocks lying in distillers' warehouses all around the country, ready to be called up as needed. It was an absolute treasure house and its worth, in both financial and gustatory sense, was enormous. Many of the malts had been long in cask and I assume Peter suggested that a better use could be found for them than being mixed in a liqueur. At the time, you may recall, the Scotch whisky industry was in one of its periodic downturns and it wasn't obvious what that better use might be. At the Scotch Malt Whisky Society we had no doubt at all that we could provide a suitable use and so an arrangement was made whereby we would purchase some of Drambuie's stocks. It was this that led, if indirectly, to the Indians coming to Dalnamain.

I had a friend called Alan, who had been lead guitar of a successful pop group some years before. The group had travelled widely and had an international reputation. It was a pretty well-known band, but Alan eventually gave up the music business to follow an unusual career path. What Alan really liked, besides music, was ancient motorbikes. Especially ancient American bikes of the Indian brand. (For connoisseurs of old American motorcycles, Indian is *the* brand. Harley Davidson is for parvenus and philistines.) Whenever he came across an Indian in his travels, Alan would buy it and eventually he assembled a respectable collection of them – most decrepit, some extremely so. He also, along the way, got to know most of the people in Europe, and some in America, who valued such things.

It is one of the more endearing characteristics of our species that very different people readily come together to form communities on the basis of a slender common interest. This was the case with Indian motorcycles, for the MacKinnon brothers shared Alan's enthusiasm, which led to the three establishing a business in which Alan would restore and sell antique Indian bikes. For premises they bought half of the mews behind our house, in which the more affluent original owners on the street had kept their coaches. Since I kept the Lagonda in a garage in the mews, this suited me very well. Not only because Alan was a good bloke, but because he installed all the machinery he might need for the rebuilding of the Indians, a matter of some interest to the owner of an old motor car which was in constant need of the sort of repair which might require the manufacture of a part from scratch.

I don't know where Alan found Willie, but he was a treasure. Not a treasure in the sense in which the Drambuie liqueur was a treasure, but a treasure nonetheless. A treasure who could be, and frequently was, difficult, Willie was an engineering machinist and an artist with metal. He was a little over five feet tall, slightly built and bow-legged, though the latter was not apparent because he had never been seen dressed in anything but a filthy boiler suit. He had very dirty fingernails; indeed his whole person seemed permeated vaguely by grime. Willie liked whisky but his preferred intoxicant was cannabis, which he took in the form of a joint which would smoulder as he pursued his calling. He persuaded Alan to buy some spectacular machine tools, which were brought with some difficulty into the lane. There was a Cincinnati milling machine of vast and ancient mien, and a massive Herbert lathe that Willie persuaded me to allow him to install in my garage for want of room in Alan's place. Of Willie's ability there could be no doubt – I see in my mind's eye a picture of him, bent over the Herbert, his joint smouldering quietly, as he turned some arcane part to a tolerance of a fraction of a thousandth of an inch.

Alan's business prospered and customers came from all over Europe, and sometimes from the USA, to buy exquisitely restored motorcycles from him, or to bring him their bikes for repair and refurbishment. The most enthusiastic of his customers came from Germany, and gradually a tradition grew up whereby the Germans would pay a visit every summer. Some would come by motorcycle, but on a modern bike, for few would subject their old machines to the rigours of such a journey. They brought their Indians in one or more large vans, which they would take to suitably scenic parts of Scotland where they would decant the machines and ride around. But one thing they deplored: the British law which prescribed that any person riding a motorcycle must wear a crash helmet, and they greatly wished to find some secluded road where they might ride free of encumbrance. Over a glass of Society whisky, Alan mentioned this to me. It provoked the emergence of a Good Idea.

'Why don't you bring them up to Dalnamain?' I suggested. Alan knew nothing of Dalnamain, so I told him. A remote spot, a long and varied single-track road which had about six vehicles a day, and a police presence for all of ten minutes every second Wednesday. Also a cottage and, if required, a supply of good whisky as well as shelter if it rained.

The following August, on a Thursday, the Indian Motorcycle Club of Germany (or some such name) arrived in Sutherland. The weather was fine and the chaps drove their bikes over the moor with their hair (those who had hair, that is) flying free. The neighbours were astonished, for a lot of the bikers looked like Vikings. The bikes and the vans were accommodated in an old barn by the bridge, and the cottage saw more and stranger folk than since the last visit by Vikings, real ones, about a thousand years ago. And the Society provided the whisky, which Alan very generously insisted on paying for.

At the time, the stove at Dalnamain was working fine. It was a massive Raeburn made of cast iron and would burn anything combustible. It had a back boiler in which it heated water, so that, in the right conditions, we could have baths in dark brown water. After the Indians left, we made the place tidy and stoked the stove, ready to be lit on our next visit, which would be some months hence. Sometimes, going down the valley, I would look back at the cottage, looking forlorn sitting high on the hillside. When I returned, at about the same spot, I would look up and say, 'At least it's still there.'

It would be four months before we returned, at the very end of December. Life had been pretty stressful and Maggie and I decided that, rather than taking part in Edinburgh's Hogmanay celebrations, which had become altogether too contrived and commercial for our taste, we would bring the New Year in quietly at Dalnamain. No crowds, indeed no people at all except ourselves seemed a desirable prospect. We little suspected that we would come close to a violent death and that our saviour would be a bottle of Society whisky.

The drive north was cold, very cold. It had been freezing for the whole week since Christmas, though no snow had fallen since Boxing Day. The main road was open and there were no reports of our road being closed, so we drove through the afternoon in hope. Our hopes were realised and the road up the valley was formally open, though there was a notice warning would-be drivers that it was not advised. The countryside was unlike anything I had seen before. It glittered: more like a Christmas card than a real landscape. It was only when we stopped at the head of the valley that we saw the cause of the glitter. The weather had been cold and dry for a week, during which ice crystals had grown to an enormous size. When we walked on the ground it was like walking on broken glass, for the huge ice crystals cracked as they broke under our feet.

Arriving late at the cottage, our one thought was to make one room warm enough to support life. We ignored the kitchen stove, which could be tricky to light, and built a big fire in the fireplace of the other ground-floor room. We slept there in reasonable comfort, though I had to get up from time to time to stoke the fire. We slept late and when we awoke we discovered two things: the fire had gone out and we had no food. (We had left in a hurry.) So we decided the best course was to get in the car and drive to the nearest town, where we might obtain coffee and supplies. This we did, but first we lit the kitchen stove. We made sure it was well alight and stoked it with wood and coals, looking forward to returning to a warm and cosy kitchen.

The coffee we got at the hotel in the town and the stores at a would-be supermarket, then headed back. We turned onto our road and, as we drove through the alder forest, I said to Maggie that we really ought to call in on Tom, a friend who lived at the foot of the valley. We did so and we took a bottle of whisky with us – for in Scotland it has long been the tradition that a caller at New Year should bring a bottle or a piece of coal, and Sutherland was a very traditional sort of place. It was, admittedly, only Hogmanay, the last day of the year, but the tradition was flexible enough for nobody to be offended, especially as the bottle we bore had a Society label – and Tom had been initiated years before.

He was delighted to see us and happy to accept our offer of a dram, followed by another. Maggie undertook to drive the rest of the way since, when we eventually managed to leave, I had had a few. I sat happily looking out of the car window at the frost and, when the cottage hove in sight, I said as usual, 'Well, it's still there.' It stayed there as we ascended the valley; Maggie parked the car and I got the shopping out of the boot. We had left the door unlocked as usual (people don't lock doors much in that part of the world) and I opened it. Or, rather, tried to open it, for something seemed to be blocking the way. I put the shopping down and forced the door open a few inches. The blockage appeared to be caused by something wedged across the passage. When we finally got in we discovered that it was the kitchen door, which by rights should have been ten feet away. The kitchen was a scene of smoking, steaming devastation. The stove had disappeared, the furniture was destroyed and all around the walls, lodged in the wood panelling were smoking coals. One window was lying in pieces on the floor and the other had vanished. As we looked around, I could discern bits of cast iron, which was all that remained of the stove. Later, I discovered a big piece of iron in the room above: it had been driven by the force of the blast through the ceiling (which was also wood-panelled) and through the boards of the floor above. There was no part of the stove which was so big that I needed two hands to pick it up.

When our shock had subsided, we realised how fortunate we had been. Judging by the still-hot coals embedded in the walls, the explosion must have happened at the most half an hour before. Had we been in the room (and we would almost certainly have been) there was no chance that we would have survived.

I later worked out what had happened. The stove had a back boiler in which it heated water. In all my tenancy of the cottage the water in the back boiler had never frozen, so there was no need to drain the system each time we left the cottage, but, because of the exceptional cold, this time the pipes had all been frozen. When the stove was alight, much of the fire's heat was transferred to the back boiler. Normally thermal circulation would have transferred this heat to the tank in the roof but with the pipes frozen, this could not happen. So: the ice in the back boiler melted to water; the water heated to become steam; the more energy was transferred from the blazing fire, the more the pressure of the steam increased until the boiler exploded. The only reason the house wasn't burnt down was that the explosion was a steam explosion. The steam blew out

92

one door and one window; when it hit the outside, where the air was about −20°C, it condensed, creating a vacuum which brought the cold air in from outside.

We spent the whole afternoon clearing up as best we could and passed the evening in the other room as before, in front of a roaring fire. We cooked on the fire and, after we had eaten, I poured two glasses of whisky. As midnight struck, I raised mine, and said to Maggie, 'A happy New Year. Enjoy the whisky, for if we had not stopped to drink from this bottle with Tom, we would not have been alive to see this New Year.'

Chapter 11

The Port o' Leith

Some years had passed since the beginning of the Society. The word had spread and then spread again. New members joined and old members renewed each year. And lots of them came to visit us, most of them delighted to be members of a club which they shared with joiners and electricians, and whose office now had a floor, if only just. We got out and about, holding whisky tastings for members and their friends and everyone thought the whisky was simply miraculous. We still struggled for stocks, for the Scotch whisky industry was still suspicious of us – or most of them were, the old ones. The younger people could see we were doing something which could only be of benefit to the whole industry, for we were creating a perception of Scotch whisky rather different from the image conveyed by traditional branded products. Sometimes I would be asked for a brief description of what we were selling. What a gift: I would reply, simply and modestly, 'That's easy. It is the best distilled liquor on the planet.' And I would challenge anyone listening to show me a spirit to compare with it. Nobody ever did.

In time our Members' Room would be completed and our patrons would have a rather classy, if eccentric, bar in which to sample Society whiskies. It was to be the scene of some memorable occasions. If it had a fault, though, it was a tendency to be a little sedate: possibly because it approximated to what a lot of the members expected: some of them thought in terms of gentlemen's clubs in Piccadilly. I tried as best I could to combat this propensity, for it wasn't conducive to fun or high jinks. In this I had the help of our head barman, the punk Dougie. This was in the 1980s, remember, and punk had by then become the badge of a recognisable lifestyle to which Dougie adhered with a commendable lack of compromise. And not only in the matter of dress: he addressed elderly members with a familiarity and friendliness which left them disoriented. He could not be faulted, though, in his knowledge of the Society's whiskies. After I left, my dull successors got rid of him, which was not only a shame, it was the waste of an asset.

For many years, I would put in an appearance on one or two evenings a week. I restricted these out of respect for my liver and because you can only spend so much of your time talking about whisky before you become repetitive and tedious. There was another reason, too. On several occasions a friend had asked me if I would like to be proposed for membership of one of the traditional gentlemen's clubs, and I had declined. In my excuses I would rarely mention the real reason, which was that I preferred the democracy of pubs to the self-selecting exclusiveness of clubs. Also, pubs were where the great stories came from.

In Leith, my favourite pub without doubt was the Port o' Leith, an ancient establishment on Constitution Street owned by my old friend Mary Moriarty. Mary was the wife (possibly the ex-wife, I never did discover) of another of my old mountaineering pals, Big Eley. Her pub was frequented by the good, the bad, the great and the small. Its barman, Jimmy, was, in local parlance, as queer as a nine-bob note, which did not in the least diminish his ability to keep order among a clientele which often included the entire crew of several ships, for the pub was known throughout the seafaring world. Only on rare occasions would Jimmy call for backup from Mary herself. Tall, well-built with a fine bosom and a tower of white hair, Mary would command obedience from the most drunken of matelots. Apocalypse then would be Mary armed with a crêpe-soled carpet slipper, a weapon to quell giants from Lithuania and toughs from Thailand alike.

One November evening the Society received a visit from a Dr McCoy who had a reputation in the United States for the greatest collection of Scotch whiskies ever amassed in North America. He had, by his own admission, more than three hundred bottles of Scotch in his den, most of which he had sampled. Since I was in the position of host I refrained from telling him what I thought of whisky collectors as a class and maintained a front of polite interest. To begin with I had hopes I might have struck a latter-day Saintsbury who would have a cellar-book of tasting notes. That would have been interesting. But alas, for my companion – as I suspect is the case for most collectors – the point of the collection was not the flavour of the whiskies but their ownership. At its best this represents a way of reifying experience: of rendering permanent something which by its nature is evanescent. At its worst, it is mere cupidity.

As you may guess, the evening dragged a bit, for my guest seemed to find the subject of Scotch – any Scotch – of inexhaustible interest. We drank a good few drams, as might be expected; the other members left; Dougie cleared glasses and bar and made a great to-do with dusters. For an hour or two I had been at a loss for an exit strategy when, possibly thanks to the drams, I had an inspiration. I told my guest about Mary and the Port o' Leith. I described Mary as the landlady with a heart of gold (which was true) and the pub as a most important centre of Scotch whisky culture (which it was not), and suggested we repair thither. Dougie, who had been listening, pointed out that it was well after closing time. But it was Saturday night, and I didn't think that likely to be too much of an impediment.

We donned coats and made our way on foot by the back of The Vaults into a maze of alleys through one of the oldest parts of the port of Leith: Dr McCoy somewhat apprehensive at what seemed to him dangerous; I perfectly at ease in what was, after all, a weel-kent part of my home town. At the end of a narrow lane the lights of Constitution Street showed themselves, and then the heavily-curtained windows of the Port o' Leith tavern. Two things were apparent to the most casual inspection: that the pub was definitely closed as far as the public was concerned, and that being closed had not diminished the jollity within. Dr McCoy stuck pretty close to my side, for it was very dark. I thumped on the side door which gave onto the alley. We waited. I thumped again and, after more time, Jimmy's face appeared round the slightly opened door. 'Oh, its yourself,' he said, opening the door wide enough to admit us.

I fear I cannot do justice to the scene within. It was one of uproarious gaiety. All the Saturday night regulars were there, in good spirits; Mary presided regally behind the bar. Songs (different songs) were being sung in several places. Though there was barely room to move, some bears from one of the oil rigs were demonstrating a dance of seemingly impossible complexity to dark-skinned persons of vaguely oriental appearance who evidently thought this simple stuff and in return pranced to an incomprehensible rhythm which their compadres provided by clapping. Presently all collapsed and would have fallen, had there been room, and another round of drinks resolved the debate. In a corner two guys, evidently deaf, played chess. We were welcomed, for there were many friends, and we were propelled, by a peristaltic motion, to the bar, where Mary had put up two whiskies. These we downed, and others after.

At some point in the early morning I piloted Dr McCoy back to the Society, where he was staying. I then forgot about the entire episode which was, after all, nothing special. That this was not the case for Dr McCoy was evident: for years after he would tell anyone who would listen about his experiences in Scotland, of which the pinnacle was, without doubt, the visit to the Port o' Leith. In the wilds of suburban Dallas this represented a connection with real life which no amount of collecting whisky might ever substitute.

One morning some months later, one of the staff told me there was a lady in the Members' Room who wanted to speak with me. It was Mary, and she was not a happy lady. It seemed there had been a spate of complaints about noise from the Port o' Leith; that the police had been called one evening and Mary, as the licensee, found to be in contravention of the conditions of her liquor licence. This was bad enough. Worse was the fact that her publican's licence was due for renewal at a forthcoming meeting of the Town Council Licensing Committee and the complainers would oppose it. At the very least she stood to lose the late licence which allowed her to stay open on Saturday nights. Was there any way I could help?

Just how I might be of assistance was not apparent, but I promised to do what I could. The first course was obviously to ascertain the facts, so I walked round to the Leith police station, which was on the corner of Constitution and Lady Charlotte Streets. I asked to see the sergeant but, since he was elsewhere, explained my mission to the constable at the counter. The constable, plainly sympathetic, promised someone would be in touch directly. I left.

I should explain a little of the social background here. Leith, as I think I have mentioned earlier, was of old a genial but rough sort of place. It was poorly lit and the streets were narrow, and what went on in them was of concern mainly to Leithers, who did not care to expose their affairs to the wider world. There was a steep social gradient, from the Georgian terraces fronting the old Links at one end to the alleys and wynds behind Bernard Street at the other. In between were tall tenements in which respectable working-class folk lived – by the standards of the time – respectable, working-class lives. But most folk had a pretty good idea of how the others lived, for they saw them every day and heard them most nights. Beginning in the 1970s, as the result of rising property values, there was a movement of middle-class people into the town, for some ancient but lovely buildings could be bought very cheaply. The incomers, fairly or not, were known to the auld residenters as the Yuppies, and a number of Yuppies had bought flats in Constitution Street. Since they were not the sort of people who would drink in the Port o' Leith, they had little notion of what went on there, or of its value in terms of human grandeur. And they thought that after ten o'clock on a Saturday night, there should be silence.

Next day, Dougie told me that there were two plods (his expression: he was no friend to the police) in the Members' Room to see me. They were the sergeant, whom I knew, and an inspector, no less. And they had come to talk to me about Mary and the Port o' Leith. It seems that the complaints had been justified. On the preceding Saturday there had indeed been a lot of noise and a battle which Mary had been unable to quell had spilled briefly onto the pavement. But the noise was the main trouble. As the sergeant said, apologetically: not only could they hear the noise at the police station (a couple of hundred yards away), but they could make out the words of the songs. And they would have to say so at the Licensing Court. This made them very sad, for when not in uniform they, too, would patronise the Port o' Leith.

We discussed the matter with all the gravity that was its due. This was an important event in the life of the port of Leith, let alone the Port o' Leith. The police would be obliged to report the facts objectively, which looked bad, but they could also say that they knew the pub to be always well-run and the locus of neither violence nor criminality. Beyond, that is, an innocent level acceptable to all civilised people. What nobody could say out loud, was that the trouble lay with the incomers and their alien values. The suggestion was that I might attend the Licensing Court as a witness to the characters of both Mary and her pub. This I agreed to do.

It was an informal affair, mainly concerned with applicants for new licences, most of which were unexceptionable. The Port o' Leith contingent was notable by its cohesion and its vivacity. I wore a business suit (my only one) and said my piece to the chairman of the court, who gave no indication that she and I had been friends for twenty years. More to the point, I presented printouts of emails from eighteen different countries, all in praise of Mary and the Port o' Leith, for I had been busy in the interim. The licence was renewed, and no word was said about Yuppies.

Chapter 12

The Tap

It has sometimes been necessary to explain to visitors a curious feature of Edinburgh pubs: the name above the door might be quite different from that by which the pub was commonly known. Thus the Forest Hill Bar was known as Sandy Bell's, and the Athletic Arms as The Diggers, from, respectively, the former proprietor, and the patrons who would drink there after finishing their shift in the adjacent cemetery. This custom induced in the citizens a certain camaraderie and a sense of their superiority to mere outsiders, for Edinburgh was a town which had a strong sense of its unique identity and, while it was not hostile to foreigners, there was a feeling that you had to earn the right to be an accepted citizen. This you did by learning the names of important things like pubs.

I was for many years a customer of a boozer of this sort on Lower Granton Road. Situated slightly below sea level just behind the harbour, it announced itself to travellers as the Granton Tavern but, in all my years of drinking there, I never heard it called anything but The Tap. Like the city, it was not unfriendly to aliens but neither did it extend a welcome, there being a feeling that merely to belong to its population was a privilege which ought to be earned. This despite – or perhaps because of – its lowly social status, for none of its regulars could be said to be affluent: but they knew who they were and they liked what they knew. What they didn't like were upper-class students, or anyone else who talked loudly and regarded them as peasants. For such folk the pub could be dangerous. Happily it was far from the usual student haunts, so visitors of that kind were rare, and those who did venture in did not repeat the experience.

For some reason I was an accepted part of the lads in the Tap and my different social and educational background were regarded as an acceptable and agreeable eccentricity. I spoke plain Scots, which helped. (The Lowland Scots language is a great leveller of social distance. Scotland is a country which for over two hundred years has suffered from an upper class which distanced itself from the hoi polloi by speaking a tortured approximation of southern English. To speak Scots by choice is consequently to declare solidarity with the mass of the people, and the people understand this.)

My preoccupation with the rebuilding of an ancient fishing boat also helped my acceptance, as did my insistence on doing all the work with my own hands. (Apart, that is from the actresses. For some years it became fashionable among young actresses to help Pip with his boat. I don't know why. I would kit them out with a boiler suit and give them a tar brush and a bucket of bitumen. None of them stayed very long but the fashion lasted long enough to tar the bottom of the *Clan Gordon*.) I had estimated the resuscitation of the boat would take eighteen months. It took ten years – more on this later.

I was keen to learn a great many things which the Tap knew about and I did not. Within the walls of the Tap were most of the craft skills which a boatbuilder might need. The Nicol brothers alone could have staffed a respectable shipyard. Joe, the eldest, was a rigger by trade – small, round, cheery, he was one of those people who, unaware of how much they know, believe that they are ignorant, which makes for modesty. Joe found it difficult to explain exactly how he made an eye splice in a laid rope, but he could make one in seconds if the rope were not too large. For hawsers he did likewise, but it took longer and involved a mighty iron fid and a hammer. His brother Davy was a plater, a skill little in demand these days. He could flame-cut steel four inches thick and leave the cut looking as though it had been machined. That skill I never learned, but I did acquire from his brother Tam the rudiments of welding with torch and electric arc. Tam was short and broad, and very muscular. He had the misfortune to look like a bruiser but be of a peaceable disposition. Alas, his appearance alone was enough to make him a target for some of the misguided youth of the adjacent housing estate, who would seek to prove their virility by assailing Tam. He would deal with them kindly and show how misguided they were with as little violence as the circumstances would admit. In the days when tattoos were to be found only on seamen and the like, Tam sported a fine depiction of a Highland piper in full dress. It was on his left bicep, which was about the size of my thigh. The execution was exquisite and every detail of the dress was discernible. Alas, it had been done by a chinaman in Hong Kong who, working from a postcard, thought from the kilt it was a picture of a lady, so threw in, at no extra cost, just above the left knee, a frilly garter.

I had developed an interest in the science of scent, the better to understand our efforts to describe the flavour of Scotch whisky. It is very far from simple and my research had taken me to some strange places and some odd smells: some good, some spectacularly awful. Easily the second worst smell I encountered was the general odour of Dr Dodd's laboratory in Inverness. George Dodd was an internationally renowned expert on olfaction and it came as something of a surprise to discover, when Maggie and I paid him a visit, that his laboratory smelt perfectly horrible. George explained gently to us that such was our power of accommodation to a constant background scent that we can block that out in favour of any variation, no matter how faint.

This knowledge was not uppermost in my mind when I met the worst-ever smell, though it did prompt some reflections later. The event occurred one Sunday afternoon in the Tap. I was sitting with Joe Nicol, each of us addressing a pint of ale, when Harry came in. Harry was a slater by trade and a gentle, grave, humorous chap by disposition. He bought a few pints and then joined us in the snug bar. As he slid onto the bench beside us, he passed something to Joe, who slipped it quickly under his jacket. My curiosity was piqued, for the action had an air of furtiveness about it which was quite foreign to the Tap. Whatever these guys might be, they were not furtive. So I turned to Joe and asked, 'What's that?'

'Oh,' he said, with a smile, 'it's mint sauce.'

Drawing the jar out, he unscrewed its lid and stuck it under my nose. Had I been sharper, I might have realised how improbable this was. But no, what I could see through the glass of the jar was greenish and fibrous, so not in conflict with the description. I took a sniff. What met me was without doubt the most disgusting and pungent odour it has ever been my misfortune to experience. I reeled and, when recovered sufficiently to breathe again, I gasped, 'Dear Christ. What's that?' Joe put the jar back in his jacket and smiled.

'It's ferret shit,' he said. 'It's for my doos.'

As explanations go, this was opaque, so I asked for particulars. Had I been more of a sleuth, I might have pieced the thing together, for I was in possession of most of the relevant facts. Harry bred ferrets, partly as pets, for they are delightful creatures, and partly for catching rabbits. They would sometimes work the warren up by my cottage at Dalnamain. Harry explained the first time he did so: 'There is no point in putting a ferret in a big warren, for the rabbits can get out all over the place and the ferret will kill inside the warren and eat a rabbit and go to sleep and you may never see him again.' Fortunately we had some small warrens of recent construction. Harry and Joe would stake little nets over all the holes and then introduce the ferret, which would disappear. Soon there would be rabbits caught in many of the nets and, if we were lucky, the ferret would come out in pursuit of a rabbit. If not, Joe would disembowel one at an upwind hole: the ferret, following the scent, would appear at the opening and be grabbed. It's a grisly business, but no more revolting than picking up your dog's shit or wiping a baby's bottom. The ferreting itself sounds pretty basic but, like so many such things, requires a degree of skill to put into operation.

The second leg on which the explanation stood was Joe's hobby of keeping racing pigeons: doves or, in Scots, doos. He had a wooden dovecot behind his council house in Granton and was inordinately proud of both doos and doocot. But Granton is next to a harbour which for hundreds of years has been frequented by ships with rats among the cargo. Rats like pigeons and are expert at penetrating dovecots: if a rat gets in, he can kill all the occupants in the course of a night. But in the hierarchy of nasty critters, ferrets are much higher-placed than mere rats and no rat which values its life will go anywhere near a ferret. Rats have an acute sense of smell, so ferret shit, sprinkled on the floor of a doocot, will deter the most intrepid of rats. It's what later came to be called biological control.

My reaction to the ferret shit did me no harm at all in the Tap. I was clearly not the first to be taken in and no doubt would not be the last. A more serious threat to my credibility was to come from an unexpected quarter. Early one winter evening, my next-door neighbour rang my door bell. Bill was, to put it very mildly, a person of unusual lifestyle. (He was, very briefly, a balding, bearded, mini-kilted, cross-dressing antiquarian and incompetent but enthusiastic amateur engineer. He had a shop in which he occasionally sold antique chandeliers.) He was a good friend and a valued neighbour. With an air of conspiracy, Bill informed me that there were some chaps in a car in the street who had for sale salmon, presumably poached or in some other way illicit. They were asking ten pounds for a fish, which was cheap for a whole salmon.

I have mentioned already that we lived in Edinburgh's Georgian New Town, an early suburb of stone, neoclassical buildings which, when we moved in, was considered scruffy but with the passage of time has come to be regarded as chic and is correspondingly expensive. The street was not well-lit, but I could see an old Ford saloon with some people in it and the boot lid raised. I strolled down. As I came to the car, I saw with some surprise that young Eddie, Harry's nephew, was in the passenger seat. Eddie blushed and affected implausibly not to have seen me. I ignored this and peered into the car boot where there appeared to be a big fish box full of dark-grey fish. A big guy whom I didn't recognise had come out of the driver's seat.

'There you are,' he said, 'new-caught fish. A tenner each. Cheap at half the price.'

I asked him to move, so that the street light might illuminate the supposed fish. They were indeed fish, and they were big. Half a dozen of them, all longer than the fish box, over whose ends they hung limply. I prodded one with a finger. My finger met little resistance and I noticed that the skin of the fish retained its impression.

'Just what is this?' I asked.

'Lovely salmon,' he replied, using the word for the first time.

Whatever they were, salmon they were not. The members of the *Salmonidae* are all notable for their silvery skin and the tightness with which it encases their flesh. The fish in the box were dark grey in colour and their flesh was flaccid. They were, besides, ugly brutes. I thanked the chap and declined the offer. Eddie kept his face averted. I returned to my door and the car drove off.

A few days later I entered the Tap, which was crowded. I was greeted with great hilarity and calls of 'Did ye like yer fish?' The story had obviously got around. I bought a few pints.

'OK,' I said to Harry. 'Tell me about it. What were those horrible fish?'

It appeared that a few of the lads were making a decent enough living by selling what purported to be poached salmon to the middle classes in the smarter parts of the town. The fish were coalfish which they bought, quite legitimately, in the fish market in the early morning for almost nothing, for the coalie is fit for cats and fishmeal and little else. It was a sweet little scam which they worked for months. Since their customers were complicit in what they believed to be illegality, there was no chance of their complaining to anyone. Oh, to have been a fly on the wall at a New Town dinner party which served coalie à la mode!

The episode did no harm at all to my standing in the Tap but I did later reflect on how precarious a thing is reputation. If I had been taken in by the scam, my position would have been uncomfortable, to say the least, and my friends would have been more embarrassed than I. As it was, Eddie was the butt of jokes for at least a week. Foremost among his persecutors was Rab, who was given to sly, ironic one-liners. There seemed to be some familial connection which privileged Rab to deliver these, but what it was I never did discover. Rab was a fixture in the Tap, where he drank Guinness, itself something of an eccentricity. Small, stooped and permanently in a state of being unshaven – which was itself a mystery before the days of designer stubble – Rab would launch his darts in an aside, his reputation for wit itself an armour. He invariably wore a flat cap; in Scots parlance, a bunnet.

Rab was an occasional lobster fisherman. That is to say, he would run a line or two of pots, forget about them for a fortnight, and then make a great effort to haul the lot and sell the contents in the fish market. (This routine was predicated on his boat engine working, which it did none too often. Happily its spasms of functionality coincided roughly with the life expectancy of lobsters in a keep pot.) Rab was generous to folk like me, who liked the miscellaneous contents of some of the pots, though my taste for whelks was not shared by my family and their boiling was banned. Rab was equable, laconic and not easily moved, so when one afternoon he entered the Tap in a state of some mental distress, our response was to buy him drink and cluster anxiously while he downed his Guinness, for we knew there must be a tale. There was. Ideally it should be told in Rab's patois but I fear that would be incomprehensible, so I will paraphrase.

Unless lobsters are very plentiful, most fishermen will keep their catch until they have enough to make it worth their while to take the brutes to the fish market. This they do in creels which they sink in the sea, the lobsters' claws held closed by rubber bands so that they are unable to rend each other. Rab kept his keep boxes off the end of Granton pier. That day, he had walked down the pier, which was deserted save for two figures which he could discern at the very end, beyond the pilots' berth. The figures appeared to be those of a man and a woman and they seemed to Rab to be in the act of taking something from a fish box and throwing it into the sea. As he got closer, he could see that they were a tall man and a woman, almost as tall, and that they were both dressed in long black coats. By the time Rab reached them, they had finished whatever they had been doing and turned as he came up.

'What are you doing?' Rab asked.

The man, who wore a dog collar, said, 'We're liberating lobsters.'

'Ye're *what?*' asked Rab incredulously.

The woman told him that God had put all creatures on earth for a reason and only Man, being vile, had seen fit to imprison them and then eat them. And the two were undoing Satan's work by liberating a box full of lobsters.

At this point in the account Rab became incoherent, so we bought him more drink and urged him to continue. Alas, he was unable to tell us exactly what was said next, but he remembered asking them where they had got the lobsters in the first place. It appears they had said in the fish market. Now Rab was nothing if not quick on the uptake, and he spotted an opportunity.

'How much did you pay for the box of lobsters?' he asked.

The man told him. Here was the germ of a beautiful idea.

'I'll do you a deal,' Rab said. 'I'm a lobster fisherman and I sell the lobsters to the fish market. If you like, we can cut out the middleman and I'll sell you them cheaper than you can get them from the fish market.'

The poets have remarked on how greed so often subverts the angelic, and Rab was all too human. He was also given to following the logic of a situation, merely for the frolic. Thus was a beautiful idea corrupted by cupidity.

Rab continued after a short pause while his interlocutors digested his proposition: 'I can dae better nor that. If you pay me for a box o' lobsters, I'll stay in the pub and no' go out and catch any. I'll dae it once a week, if you like.'

We crowded round. 'What did he say?' asked a dozen voices.

It sounded like 'Bugger off,' but, as I say, I paraphrase.

A few pints of Guinness later Rab, his morale restored, returned to the pier end where he dropped six baited lobster pots. He said he caught the lot in two days. And, for lack of any other buyer, sold them at the fish market.

CHAPTER 13

Simon's Bulldozer

If anything lay at the core of the Society it was the Tasting Committee: half a dozen guys sitting round a table, charged with describing the flavour of whiskies. This had to be (and was) productive of a lot of fun. That it comprised only men was not the result of any conscious sexism: more an accident – and I don't recall any strident demand from the women of my acquaintance to join it. 'We'll let that flee stick tae the wa,' as the old Scots saying goes, for it is not my intention in what follows to advert to sexual politics.

Because the Tasting Committee was fun, it occurred to us quite early that our members might like to do something similar, and out of that was born the notion of tasting whisky as an amusing activity in itself. As far as I know, nobody else had ever thought of doing such a thing. We would set out whisky in glasses, then one of our people would inspect the whiskies one by one, commenting on the flavours: first on the nose, then on how the stuff tasted and finally on the aftertaste. Members would be encouraged to talk about the whisky and generally enjoy the occasion. Unlike a professional tasting, nobody would spit the spirit out so the event would soon become quite convivial. It was a great success when first we tried it and we would soon be doing it around the country, usually at smart venues, some of them very smart indeed.

Attendance at the events was restricted to members and their guests, which created a familial atmosphere and strengthened the social aspect of the Society. While the intention was perfectly serious, nobody was pompous and nobody was made to feel a low being just because they couldn't perceive a soupçon of jasmine beneath the surface phenolics. There soon evolved a regular programme of tastings nationwide, and members looked forward keenly to them. The members of the Society again proved to be its most effective advertisement and it wasn't long before members were asking if we would lay on a whisky tasting, not for members in general, but for a group of their friends or colleagues – people who weren't members of the Society but, if all went well, might become so. There could be no reasonable objection to this and so grew a trend for us occasionally to provide a whisky tasting as a leisure activity.

It is a world with which I have little acquaintance, but I understand that many big corporations lay on a sort of holiday as a reward for their staff for doing well, or as an incentive to do better. For tax reasons the purpose of this is often obscured and I believe that the Inland Revenue acquiesces in the deception, though an afternoon of paintball warfare in a wet wood might be hard to class as a perquisite. From time to time, usually because one of our members sat on an entertainments committee, we would receive a request to lay on a tutored whisky tasting as part of an incentivising weekend. It wasn't my favourite way to spend an afternoon or evening but, grumbling, I would, if my arm were twisted.

One day in June 1987, my friend Tim Steward and I, having been thus coerced, made our way to a big country house in Fife (Tim was now one of our directors). The place was agreeable, as were the staff, and so were the prospective whisky tasters, so we soon relaxed into the spirit of the thing. The tasters-to-be were middle to senior executives of some conglomerate company, I forget which. Tim had brought nosing glasses (essential for an accurate inspection of a whisky) sufficient for the estimated numbers, plus a good many extra – which was fortunate, for it seemed that almost all the people had preferred the whisky to the paintball alternative, which raised them in our estimation. The whole thing went well for about an hour and a half, after which the formal proceedings dissolved into cheerful chat and promiscuous downing of drams.

I was blethering away to a group when one of the tasters came up to me and detached me with a request that I would join his group. This I did. He then said, 'You don't remember me, do you?' I looked closely at him; the face was familiar, but dimly in the distant past.

'I'm Simon,' he said. 'Scuba diving, Loch Sween, the bulldozer.'

At that the mists cleared and I remembered perfectly. He turned to his friends excitedly and said, 'This is the man. This is the guy I have been telling you about, who stole the bulldozer.'

It wasn't quite true. It was a digger, not a bulldozer, but Simon had evidently told the story often, for they all knew what he was talking about. I then had to tell the tale, so I may as well tell it to you, though it was nothing to get excited about.

Many years before, when I was young and breath came easily, I had taken up scuba diving. Those were in the early days (relatively speaking) when breathing sets had become common enough but the technology was still evolving. (I generally used a twin-hose Siebe Heinke demand valve, the sort of thing that nowadays you might see on the wall of a dive-gear shop as an interesting antique.) Popular interest in diving had grown to the point at which Edinburgh University had allowed a sub-aqua club to be set up for those of its students who wished to participate. But the university was a bit nervous, because in some distant waters one or two divers had recently been drowned or injured by the bends, and the university was aware that drowned students were bad news. It therefore encouraged a bunch of guys who were doing PhDs, most of them engineers, to run the Edinburgh University Sub-Aqua Club and, in return for not drowning undergraduates, it furnished the club with a lot of expensive gear including a compressor, a big Zodiac boat and an outboard motor, as well as pretty good breathing sets. At the urging of some of my friends (the engineering PhDs) I had joined the club.

We usually met on a Thursday evening in a pub, to plan whatever we would do at the weekend. One Thursday (it was exam time) the only two of us in the pub were Simon and me, both of us keen to go diving the following evening. I made a suggestion to which Simon, who was much younger, agreed: namely that we should go to the west coast, to Loch Sween, where a friend of mine had a caravan which we could use. There was a recently-discovered wreck in the Sound of Jura that I wanted to take a look at. It was quite deep – about fifty metres – but it would be useful decompression training for Simon. There was a boat, too, though we wouldn't need that, for we would take the club inflatable.

The caravan on Loch Sween warrants a little explanation. I had a friend called John Godfrey who was a biologist and who lectured in the university. In the halcyon days (as we came to see them) of the sixties, John had devised a scheme to study naturally-occurring genetic variation in field voles. Don't ask why, for I have no idea, but the proposal must have had some merit for the Nuffield Trust gave John the funds to do the study over a period of twenty years. It involved taking an existing population of voles, splitting it into five parts, isolating the parts from one another and then looking to see what happened. John needed five places where his populations of voles could be kept separate, but in a uniform natural environment. He found an ideal location at the head of Loch Sween, a sea loch which penetrates deeply into the land, and which has a number of small islands, none of them with a natural population of voles.

The funding for the study covered the purchase of a Land Rover to travel between Edinburgh and Tayvallich, a small motor launch to travel among the islands and a caravan to live in while engaged in the study. John made a good choice in the last two: the launch was a small cabin cruiser with a twin-cylinder Kelvin diesel engine, and the caravan was an old showman's caravan, complete with cut-glass curtained windows and a fine enamelled cast-iron stove. Because he was a respectable academic, the Forestry Commission gave John permission to park his caravan on their land, on the very shore of the loch, in dense conifer forest. There was no need for security, for the Forestry owned all the land for miles around and the caravan was at the end of a three-mile track, which you turned onto from the road, itself only a single-carriageway some five miles from Bellanoch. The latter isn't exactly a metropolis, having a garage and three houses. John knew little about boats and I did what maintenance was needed in return for the occasional use of the caravan and the boat.

Simon and I had agreed to meet at the club lockup on Friday at teatime. I would bring a car which we would use to tow the club inflatable on its trailer. He was a bit surprised, but pleased, when I turned up in the Lagonda. It was wet, but that didn't cause us any grief; if you are to do anything at all out of doors in the west of Scotland, you can't let a bit of rain stop you. We loaded the gear, hitched up the trailer and set off in the gathering dark and the rain. Now, as you know from earlier, rain and darkness was a bad combination for the Lagonda, for the generator attached to the Gardner engine wasn't quite up to running headlamps and windscreen wipers at the same time.

(The headlamps were huge things, with one big bulb in each. To dip the beam, the whole lamp tilted forward and pointed at the road.)

It's a long haul from Edinburgh to Loch Sween: by Glasgow to Loch Lomond, up the side of the loch and by Rest-and-be-Thankful to the head of Loch Fyne, then via Inveraray and Lochgilphead to the Crinan Canal – in those days a good five or six hours' driving. I was concerned about the car's batteries but there wasn't much I could do about it, so trusted to luck. (You might think that, given my history, I should long ago have given up on luck, but no.) We got there in the end: Simon a little apprehensive as the forest closed in; a little more so when we turned off onto the dirt road which ran through the forest to the hollow by the lochside where lay the caravan. However, a good fire in the stove and a dram of whisky cheered him up. We slept well that night. In the morning we decided, since it was still wet, to go to Crinan for some breakfast. We unhitched the trailer which we had rather abandoned the night before. At that point, not before, I remembered my apprehensions about the Lagonda's generator. They were justified. The engine gave a slight groan in response to the starter, and gave up. The batteries were flat.

If I had had a little sense, I would have parked the car on a little hill nearby, which would allow me to bump start it – for as you may recall, it had a diesel engine and a diesel will run without electricity, provided you can get it going. And, once going, with no untoward demands on it, the generator would soon recharge the batteries, but there was absolutely no way of starting it. You couldn't swing a four-litre Gardner with a starting handle if it had had a starting handle, which it didn't. I was thus at a standstill. Simon asked whether the boat might have a battery which we could borrow. I said alas, no, it had a little Kelvin which *could* be started by hand. We made some tea and considered. I announced that there was nothing for it, we must walk to Bellanoch and persuade the garage owner to rescue us. How ignominious.

Happily the rain had cleared and we set off on the forestry track. About a couple of miles up the track, we came to a big clearing where several tracks met. There were several vehicles, including a bulldozer and a digger, and quantities of road-building materials. It was Saturday afternoon and there was nobody about.

I stopped and said cheerfully, 'Look, our problem's solved.'

Simon looked blank. 'What do you mean?' he asked.

I pointed at the roadmaking vehicles. 'We'll borrow one of those and tow the Lagonda until it starts.'

'Oh,' said Simon.

I prowled round the bulldozer and the digger. The dozer was fairly new but, though I hadn't had much experience of driving dozers, I knew them to be very slow. I turned my attention to the digger: a JCB with a shovel at the front and a backhoe at the rear. It was old, which meant there was probably little in the way of locks: certainly nothing formidable. It did have an ignition lock, though, which Simon pointed out. He also pointed out that we had no key.

'That's all right,' I said. 'Look for a length of wire, two or three feet.'

'What sort of wire?' he asked.

'Any kind of wire,' I replied. 'Electric cable if you can find it; fence wire would do.'

Simon went looking for wire while I inspected the machine. I could, if pushed, extract the wiring from the lock, but that would give us away, and on John's behalf I didn't want to offend the Forestry Commission who were, after all, his landlords. The digger's engine had been stopped by a strangler, but that I returned to its default position. Then Simon came back with some fence wire. It was the work of a few minutes to connect the starter motor to a positive battery lead, and a few minutes more to find out how to steer the thing and which levers (there were lots of them) worked which bits of the digger. Having done that, I told Simon to jump on board, which he did.

I expect there is a reason why diggers don't have springs. Maybe ours was just old and tired, but the journey back to the car was bumpy – and with its shovel and backhoe, its steering was terrible. Simon was delighted and said he was enjoying the ride. He was less pleased when, having got to the car and connected it by a towrope to the back of the digger I said, 'Right, Simon. Which do you want to drive, the car or the digger?'

After a second's consideration, he said that since he had never driven a digger, it would have to be the car. So, having opened the Lagonda's driver's door, I told him to get in. It was then that he looked at his feet.

'What's with the pedals?' he asked.

I pointed out that the pedals were as is usual in cars with a manual gearbox: clutch, brake and accelerator pedal. It was just that instead of being on the right, the accelerator pedal was in the middle with the brake to its right. And I explained about the flyoff handbrake which at the least touch would do just that, fly off. Then I showed him how he should start the engine once I had got him under tow.

'Return the strangler to the run position, set the hand throttle to low, use the lever on the steering column to retard the fuel injection, engage third gear and let the clutch in. OK?'

Simon said, 'Um,' in a non-committal way.

'As soon as it starts, which will be almost immediately, put it out of gear and wave your hand at me. Or sound the horn if there is enough juice in the batteries.' (There wasn't.) 'I will stop the digger. You stop the car, be sure to use the pedal on the right, and apply the handbrake, which will stay on if you press the button on top.'

It all worked beautifully: the car started, I stopped, so did Simon who also managed not to stall it. I disconnected the towrope and drove the car onto the little hill, where it could safely run down to start again. We returned the digger to exactly the spot where we had left it. I thought of leaving a note saying thanks for the use of your digger but decided against it. Simon was delighted. It seems he had been telling the story ever since, to anyone who would listen.

The search for the wreck however wasn't a success. Viewed from below, the sea is a much bigger place than it looks when seen from above. The traditional method of locating yourself by cross-bearings on landmarks is fine for most coastal navigation in good weather, but pretty hopeless when you are on the bottom and the visibility is about thirty feet, so we didn't find the wreck. What we did find was a very large lobster, walking on the shingle fifty metres down, where no self-respecting lobster has any reason to go. Grabbing him was easy enough but getting him to the surface in a process that involved stopping twice on a shotline to decompress was somewhat difficult, especially since the lobster appeared to be unhappy about being grabbed and was trying to get at me with his claws. And, being so big, he was pretty tough eating.

In the event we had taken John's boat, rather than the inflatable, and that gave trouble too – though the trouble wasn't unexpected and was the main reason for giving the engine a trial run. A Kelvin of that sort was cooled by seawater which ran through passages in the gearbox and engine: it was a reliable system but vulnerable to blockages. When we got back I dismantled the thing and examined its transfer passages but could find no trace of deposited material. I even poked around inside the engine with a screwdriver, but all I met was the shiny black of the cast-iron block. That left me without an explanation, even though I thought about it for a fortnight. Then business took me to Glasgow, so I phoned Kelvin, the makers, and arranged to pay them a visit. Kelvin was an engineering company which had been building marine engines for over a hundred years. The engines ranged all the way from John's little boat to ocean-going ships, so my enquiry was small beer. The premises were a course of low buildings fronting onto a street called Dobbie's Loan. I was received politely and ushered by a young lass into a waiting room with two seats in it. After a few minutes a man in a tweed jacket came in and said, 'You better come into the office and tell us what it's about.' He led me through a door into an office which might have done for a film set for *Dombey and Son*; but no director would have accepted it: it was too preposterously ancient and disorderly. It was a big room with four or five desks around the walls. On those walls were pictures of ships and engineering drawings of parts of engines. In the middle of the room was a big dining table covered with papers. The papers had reached what I believe geologists call the angle of rest. That is, their condition was such that, if anything were added to the top, it would precipitate a slide which would cause something to slide off the bottom. The man asked me what the trouble was. I told him. He then said, 'You had better ask Archie,' and led me to a door which opened off the main office. Inside there was a small room with a desk, slightly tidier than its big brother outside, but not much. Behind the desk, a big man sat in shirt-sleeves. On the walls, more engineering drawings, two of which were blueprints.

Archie smiled and gestured toward a seat. 'Right,' he said. 'What's the trouble? And first, what kind of an engine are we talking about?'

I said, 'It's a P2 diesel, and it's overheating.' I then described the symptoms and the results of my investigations.

Archie thought for a little and then asked, 'Where is your boat lying?'

I couldn't see what this had to do with it, but told him, 'Loch Sween.'

'In that case', he said, 'your problem's mud. Mud hard-caked in the transfer passages.'

I got a strong impression that if I had said the boat was lying in the Irrawaddy, he would have been able to give a diagnosis. I pointed out that I had searched the passages and all I could find was clean cast iron. Archie smiled.

'I know,' he said, 'it looks like cast iron and feels like cast iron, but hit it with a cold chisel and you'll find it's mud. In a place like Loch Sween it cakes hard and you have to chip it away.'

I left, far from happy, but at least there was no charge for expert opinion. It was some weeks before I again headed west. Despite my scepticism, I did as I had been told and, having stripped the engine down, attacked it with a cold chisel and a hammer. Sure enough, it was mud. I sent him a letter of thanks and contrition, together with a bottle of whisky.

Chapter 14

Walkabout

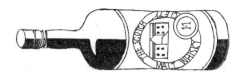

Toward Christmas that year I was feeling restive, so decided to visit a relative: a distant relative at the periphery of a very extended family. When my sister lived with him, I described Dick Morton as my common-law brother-in-law, referring to an old Scots custom of marriage by habit and repute. After she left him, in Papua New Guinea's capital, Port Moresby, I called him my former common-law brother-in-law, which I thought was rather neat. He and Marion remained ever after on affectionate terms, but she had got on a plane to London directly after he had had his face tattooed by some of his cannibal pals up in the Baliem Highlands – though whether because of that, I never did discover.

Dick was an officer and a gentleman and, though he tried hard, he was never able to disguise the fact. Though his dress was bizarre and his tattoos spectacular, nobody was deceived, and if you had had to guess as to his history and you suggested a Wiltshire estate, Rugby, Cambridge and the 7th Hussars, you wouldn't have been far wrong. But you might not have guessed that he was a serious geneticist. At the time I first met him, he had resigned his position as a don and taken the lowly post of research assistant, that being the least prestigious job that would allow him access to his laboratory. His rejection of his English upper-class status was as complete as it was traditional. He was an expert on tropical agriculture, and he was a good and generous man who had been friends with the Cuban revolutionaries in the sixties. I have known many folk who drove scruffy cars, but Dick's was the only one which had grass growing in it.

At the time, he and his grown-up son Dan were the proprietors of a huge coconut plantation called Undine Bay in Vanuatu. If you don't know where Vanuatu is, you are not alone. Very roughly, if you leave the top right-hand edge of Australia behind and head northeast across the Pacific by jet for about three hours, you will come to what was called the New Hebrides, and is now Vanuatu. It is a string of volcanic islands, all of them tropical and the more northerly ones equatorial. The people are Melanesians, which is to say that, by European standards, most of them seem very black and rugged – though it only takes a week or two on the islands for one's perception of such things to alter remarkably. The islands themselves are lovely. I think all of them began their existence as volcanoes and then acquired a few million years' accretion of coral. Some of the islands still have active volcanoes, which, besides Dick, was one of my reasons for visiting.

The flight is one of the longest you can take if you are travelling with a purpose, as opposed to just travelling. My itinerary was Edinburgh, London, Newark, Honolulu, Sydney, Brisbane, Port Vila. I prepared for it well. I had a satchel slung over my shoulder and a leather flight case containing a dozen bottles of Society whisky. As far as Newark there were no problems, but when I went to board the Continental Airlines flight for Sydney, they said that as I had no Australian visa, they wouldn't carry me. My retort, that I had relatives there, sounds limp now.

I had never been to Australia and my knowledge of the country had been gleaned from an inherited family stamp album which contained lots of Australian stamps with Queen Victoria's head on them. None of this cut any ice and I was firmly told, 'no visa, no seat'. Then I had a good idea. I said, 'Can't you carry me as far as Hawaii at least? Isn't it in the United States?' I hadn't been there either but what little I knew of the place (gleaned from American movies) suggested it might be a more fun place than Newark. Guardedly they said yes, but I would be bumped half way.

I was. At ten o'clock the next evening (or maybe the same evening, it's hard to be sure) I found myself with satchel and case of whisky sitting on a bench in Honolulu airport. Now you might think that would be no bad thing but, let me tell you, Honolulu airport at 2200 hours is like Stavanger on a Sunday. Nothing is open: no shops, no bars, no restaurants. The only thing moving is the taxi queue and that stops as soon as a flight has come or gone. There seemed little prospect of an Australian consul willing to issue me with a visa on demand, so I decided to take a taxi to a hotel. Then I realised I had a problem: I had no US dollars and all the currency exchanges were shut. I did have a dozen bottles of whisky, but there was no obvious way of translating them into a bed for the night.

I wandered over to the taxi rank and spoke to the driver of the first cab. I explained my predicament and suggested, without much hope of success, that he might take me to a hotel where I could change some currency with which to pay him. To my surprise he said 'OK, jump in.' I did, and he drove off toward town. He was a Filipino who had only recently become a US citizen. As we drove along, he explained just how important citizenship was to him and to his many dependants back in the Philippines. He didn't make much money and he worked long hours, but as long as he paid his taxes and obeyed the law, he would be free to do as he pleased with his profits and his life.

As he spoke, I came to realise that what I had taken for granted all my life was to him a treasured privilege. The freedom from arbitrary arrest and extortion, common in democratic countries, was for him the greatest good imaginable. As he drove up to the rather grand entrance of the Holiday Inn Honolulu, I asked him to wait, saying I would leave my bags as a surety for my return with some US dollars to pay my fare. He waved me away. 'Have the ride on me,' he said. 'Say something good about America.' I have done so, many times, and whenever I have told this story, especially in the US, I have found myself among friends.

I dined the next night in the hotel. I am fond of seafood and the buffet was easily the most spectacular display of assorted crustaceans I have ever seen: the centrepiece an enormous Pacific spider crab, and lots of green-lipped mussels, which were then to be found only on the Pacific littoral. I think I have never been so disappointed in my life: it had all been over-cooked to the point at which the flesh had the consistency of cotton wool, and about as much flavour. I spoke to the waiter, who didn't appear to understand what I was saying; then to the chef, with no more success. The management proved elusive and when I eventually secured an interview with someone in authority, he seemed disinclined to do anything about it, saying only that nobody had complained before. I ended up eating vegetables and feeling grumpy. At least they didn't charge me for my dinner. Just by way of contrast, the next day I lunched on the north side of the island, at a shack the size of a garden shed, run by two Koreans. The food was utterly delicious and the meal one I shall remember with gratitude as long as I live.

The Aussie visa took a couple of days, then Continental again to Sydney and a short internal flight to Brisbane. No worries, as they say in Oz. Fat chance, as they say in Govan. About a couple of hours out the pilot asked for seatbelts to be fastened and told us we would be skirting the edge of a minor typhoon. Nothing to worry about, he said. I had a window seat at the rear, with a good view of the starboard wing, which seemed to be behaving oddly. In my experience aircraft wing tips generally remain more-or-less stationary with respect to the fuselage. This one didn't. It waggled up and down as it sped through the dark and the driving rain. This I deplored but stoically resolved to say nothing, assuming the pilot would know. Just then, the whole craft dropped like a stone through several thousand feet.

It was not a good night and I was not my sprightly best in Sydney the next morning. My mood did not improve when the man at the Australian customs told me I would have to pay duty on twelve bottles of whisky and the duty was proportional to the alcohol content, which in this case was about 60%. He regarded me as I expect he would had I declared a few kilos of heroin. I protested that I wasn't going to drink the whisky in Australia, nor would I use it to corrupt the famously abstemious Australian populace. I only wanted to take it with me to Brisbane and then goodbye to Oz. He didn't budge: either I pay some astronomical sum or he would impound my whisky. I have occasionally found that when in trouble in a public place, shouting can be an effective tactic. (I once used this to effect in the old Soviet Union, though if I had known how risky it was, I would have kept quiet.) But in Sydney I thought it might work, so I demanded very loudly to speak to a superior officer. Arrest seemed imminent, I think what saved me was the sheer respectability of my cargo. All Australians like Scotch whisky and it follows that any bearer of it must be an OK person – even if it is so strong that a glass of the stuff would slay a wombat.

A senior official appeared and demanded to know the cause of the fuss. I relaxed as soon as I heard the tones in which his demand was couched, for he spoke in broad Scots. I explained my predicament, which he appeared to think less problematic than did his minions. He asked where I was from, not, as you might think, enquiring where had I boarded the inbound flight. In Lowland Scots, the phrase refers to your place of birth or upbringing. I told him. He said, 'I'm frae Bonnybridge. Do you ken Jake Highett? Or Bob Busby or George Clark?'

They were all old mountaineers, 'Yes,' I said. 'All of them. And their mate Arthur Ferguson, who saved my life after I fell off the Horrible Hook.'

Furthermore the chap had heard of the Scotch Malt Whisky Society, and had pals who were members. An arrangement was accordingly made, whereby my case of bottles was sealed and certified, and transferred directly to the Brisbane flight. From that it went onto the Port Vila aircraft, though into the hold because the plane was too small for it to go in the cabin. The latter had about a dozen seats down either side, each with a window, but little in the way of overhead lockers. There was one air hostess who, about an hour into our flight, issued us with landing cards and explained about entry into the sovereign state of Vanuatu. One item caught my attention: the import of alcohol was limited to one bottle of spirits per passenger. Anything beyond that was liable to a horrific rate of duty. (It turned out that Vanuatu had no direct taxes at all. No Income Tax, no capital taxes of any sort, which made it popular with rich expats, but left the country dependent on import duties for its revenue.) So my whisky presented a problem yet again.

By that time I had made the acquaintance of my fellow-passengers who numbered about eight or nine, all youngish men. They were geologists, employees of some big mining corporation, and they were going to Vanuatu to prospect for gold. It seems some small deposits had been found and an aerial reconnaissance suggested that a proper survey might disclose more. The chaps weren't too pleased about their trip, Christmas being close, but it seems some bigwig had given an order. None of them were carrying any liquor, so all offered to carry a bottle for me. In return I invited them all to the Undine

Bay Christmas Party. I didn't know for sure that there would be a party, but I knew Dick of old and I didn't foresee a problem. The whole thing worked perfectly. I paid duty on only two bottles and a few weeks later we all had a great time drinking the finest malt whisky alternated with coconut shells of kava.

The airport at Port Vila was something of a shock after Heathrow, Newark and Honolulu. There was a tarmac runway but not much else. The terminal seemed to be a collection of shacks. And it was hot, very hot, and humid, so that the sweat started running down your back within a few minutes of leaving the plane, which you did by a ladder. A lot of big black guys offered to carry bags, but I held onto mine. I wasn't taking any chances at this stage of the journey. The jetlag had something to do with it, for by that time I was somewhat limp. It was dark, but among the crowd I easily discerned the tall, lean figure with the shock of hair. Dick, good man, was waiting. I introduced the prospectors and told about the Christmas Party. Dick rose to the occasion, as I had known he would.

'No problem,' he said. 'All welcome. And we can find beds for the lot of you, no worries.' (His long stay in the Antipodes had evidently affected his hitherto rather posh English.)

We found a bar. Dick parked the pick-up and told me to throw my bags in the back. I told him the case was full of whisky and suggested we take it with us.

'Not a problem,' he said. 'There is no crime of that sort in the islands. If it were a pig, mind you, I would have asked you to bring it into the bar.'

The bar appeared to be of the kind in which pigs might be welcome. We had a few beers with the geologists and then headed out into the night, which was very black. After about a mile, the street lamps ceased and so did the tarmac. The road appeared to be cut through dense vegetation. It was not a bad one, as dirt roads go, but not comforting either. I was pretty wrecked and after about an hour Dick suggested we pause for a refreshment. Given the circumstances the circumlocution seemed odd, but I sleepily assented. A mile or two later, in a canyon of even thicker jungle, Dick braked and pulled to a halt.

'Drink,' he said. Then he switched the lights off.

At first the darkness seemed total. I opened the pick-up door and stepped out, trusting that I would find something to step onto. Surprisingly, there was a road. Only when I looked up could I gather some sense of how things were, for overhead was a strip of blazing stars, framed on either side by vegetable walls. As my eyes adjusted, I saw that beside the road, a metre or so from the ground, there was a tall yellow flame. It was a piece of bamboo, the top segment of which had been filled with kerosene, a rag put in and lit.

'Pub sign,' said Dick. 'Follow me.'

In the black-green wall behind the flame there appeared to be a passage into which he plunged. There was nothing for it but to follow. About fifty yards in, I could make out another light and beyond that, another still. Keeping close to Dick, I shortly found myself in a small clearing in which I could discern by the light of some more rags, a shack whose walls and roof were of pandanus leaves. Within the shack, at the back, there was a bench, on which sat three of the most villain-ous-looking human beings I have ever seen. (I have said that by our standards Melanesians are not pretty. These guys would, I thought, have graced the towers of Notre-Dame.)

To the left of the door, in the dimness, I could make out a big man standing behind a small table. Under the table there was a bucket and clamped on it, directly over the bucket, a mincer. I squinted, took off my specs, cleaned them with a handkerchief and looked again. It was indeed a mincer, of the sort that few people now use but everyone has in a kitchen drawer. I would as soon have expected a trombone. Dick invited me to have a seat and proceeded to explain that it was indeed a mincer and it was used to prepare the drink with which we would presently be served. The chap at the table picked up from the floor what looked like a rather dirty root and stuffed it into the mincer, turning the handle as he did so. The whitish, minced root fell into the bucket. When it was all through, water was poured over and the whole lot stirred with a stick. The mess was ladled into half-coconut shells, which were placed, wobbling, on the table.

Dick then delivered a short homily on the subject of etiquette – which was, to put it mildly, unexpected. He said, 'I should have told you about this before, but I didn't think. The root the fellow was mincing is called kava. It grows locally and is perfectly legal. I have analysed it in the lab. It's very complicated; it has some of the characteristics of the hallucinogens and is in some ways like an opiate, but very mild, and you needn't worry about taking it. But you have to show good manners.' (This – bizarrely in the circumstances – put me in mind of my Auntie Peggy, a long-dead Glaswegian housewife, who was very strong on manners.)

He went on, 'The stuff in the shells tastes pretty disgusting. So bad, in fact, that the custom is to take your drink, walk a few steps away from the company, knock it back in a oner, recompose your features and return to the fold. OK?'

Just then one of the gargoyle-like denizens of the shed did just that. I had to admit that when he returned, he seemed a touch more genial than before. I did as I had been told, for I trusted Dick and I knew that there were few folk more knowledgeable about the pharmacology of intoxicants than he, and fewer still with his direct experience of them.

I took my half shell, turned my back to the company and raised the cup to my lips. It smelt like swamp water with a soupçon of drains. I gagged. And then I took the plunge. It didn't taste as bad as it smelled, which wasn't saying much, but the effect was almost immediate. The dank jungle metamorphosed very slightly, the leaves shimmered a little and the creepers appeared to have been draped by an interior designer. The denizens of the shack seemed kindly old gentlemen, solemn but benevolent. I felt peaceful and my weariness dropped away as though it were a thing which I must carry, but not in haste.

Come the dawn, Undine Bay lay beneath us. Green hills formed a semicircle filled with improbably tall coconut palms: the centre some low white buildings and the diameter a line of coral strand beyond which the turquoise of the shallows gave way to the deep pelagic blue of the ocean. The road dropped down the slope and the jungle wall turned into lines of palms. Dick drew up in front of the building nearest the sea: a big colonial bungalow raised on stilts a metre or so above the ground. In front of the house, betraying its European origins, was a stretch of green in which close-planted succulents did service unconvincingly for lawn. Beyond that was a glaring white coral beach. Dan, Dick's son, came down the steps to welcome us.

'Good morning,' he said. 'Would you like some breakfast?'

He apologised for the informality, explaining that he was on his way to work, hence the clothing. There was little enough of that: Dan would spend the next hour horse-breaking and his working gear consisted of a Stetson hat against the sun, shorts, long boots and leather chaps: the latter the sort of things people used to wear in cowboy films. He was later to explain that for tropical horse handling this was the only sensible sort of wear. The island had been colonised in the nineteenth century by British settlers who had brought with them hunters rather than work horses – though what they expected to hunt, nobody knows, for foxes were as common as polar bears. The hunters had escaped and themselves colonised the uninhabited volcanic centre of the island where they now formed a large feral population. There was little groundwater higher up, so the ponies came down to the lowland to drink, where Dan caught them and tamed them. The latter he did by feeding and friendship and sweet talking: he was a professional, and explained that nobody who wanted a trustworthy work horse would use the bronco-busting method you used to see in the movies.

So, your actual tropical paradise. At seven every morning I would cast off my mosquito net, trot across the lawn and the beach, and dive into the milk-warm sea. Lying on my back I would watch the sun rise behind the mountain. Then, lying on my front, gaze down among the coral trees and badly designed fish in iridescent, lurid colours. So far, so good, but with only a snorkel and a mask I felt deeply vulnerable. (If you have breath for about a minute, you are ill-prepared to deal with anything nasty that comes round a corner. With scuba gear and a big knife you may not be much safer, but you surely feel you are.) Dick had told me that inshore I wouldn't meet any sharks worse than reef white-tips and I did bump into a few of those, one literally. But, he added on the first evening, there were tigers out in the deeper water and I should keep a lookout lest any of them came inshore. How you keep a lookout for a shark that is travelling as fast as those brutes do, in water where the visibility is about fifty feet, I don't know. The only consolation is that you probably won't know when it happens, for an attack by a tiger shark is like being hit by a travelling bandsaw.

A week or two of idleness left some vivid impressions. Sitting in the dark one evening, perfectly naked and up to the neck in warm seawater in a volcanically heated rock pool, drinking gin and tonic. Or the morning I went for a walk to the perimeter hedge. 'Hedge' is a word which suggests the prim privet of suburbia, or at worst some berberis. The tropical equivalent is about thirty feet high, perfectly opaque and armed with thorns that make you think kindly of chainsaws. But, this being paradise of a sort, there was an upside, in the shape of a mango tree. I smelt it before I saw it. Big, with lots of branches bearing dark-green leaves and hundreds of mangoes in various states of ripeness. I had never seen a mango tree before and I was delighted. I climbed into the greenness and, about thirty feet up, found a comfortable-looking crook in which I sat, my back against the bole. I then picked the most perfect-looking fruit and, peeling it with my pocket knife, ate it. With the sweetness of the juice running down my chin and the dappling of the light through the leaves, that was as close to bliss as I ever expect to come.

One evening, as we ate steaks from one of the horses which had been deemed more suited to the pot than it was to hard work, I raised the ostensible purpose of my visit, a trip to a volcano.

Dick considered this for a while, then said, 'There are plenty to choose from. We could go north up to Pentecost, where there are several, but I think it might be better to take a trip down to Tanna. I've never been there, but I get good reports of the island and the people – and the volcano is reasonably accessible. What is more, they say that the best kava in the islands – which means the best in the world – grows on Tanna.

'And,' he went on, 'I have a pal who is a big buddy of the chief and will give us an introduction.'

Transport for the trip was what an earlier century would have called a tramp steamer. The one we took had a big Cummins diesel but was otherwise straight out of a Joseph Conrad novel. Not large – a few hundred tons – and what it lacked in paint it made up for in rust. A wheelhouse, a hold and a derrick served by a very large winch appeared to be the principal features on deck, other than a strange boat made of heavy-gauge steel plate and as rusty as its parent. No doubt there was more below deck but that was not visible, for there appeared to be no provision at all for the passengers. It was certainly democratic.

It would take about eighteen hours to get to Tanna, weather permitting, with one stop at an island called Erromango. We settled down on some rather comfortable cargo nets beside three large ladies, several children and two pigs. The ladies handed round sweetmeats and mangoes, and evidently regarded us much as they did the children. Dick conversed with them in Bislama, the Vanuatu version of Pidgin. He had been expert in Tok Pisin in Papua New Guinea, he explained, and this wasn't too different and easy to pick up. Being based on English, it was, and after a few weeks on the islands I found I could make myself understood – mostly. Dick also told me about the religions we could expect to meet. It appears that when in the nineteenth century missionaries were sent to save the souls of the people of the New Hebrides, several brands of Christianity arrived about the same time. Because there were so many islands and so few missionaries some sort of ecumenical spirit prevailed and now the folk up in Pentecost were all Roman Catholics whereas in Erromango, our first stop, they were Presbyterians.

'You should feel at home, being Scotch,' Dick said.

We didn't stop long enough at Erromango for me to find out much about its history or religion, which may be just as well, for the island's experience of foreigners was not such as to encourage a contemplation of either. Its population depleted by slavers and its psyche depressed by American evangelical missionaries, it had no reason to present a friendly face to the outside world, let alone produce the smiles with which we were greeted.

Tanna was another matter. The island, lush, forested and mountainous, looked inaccessible from seaward, as indeed it was, having then no harbour, natural or artificial. We went ashore in the rusty boat, which performed surprisingly well in the Pacific swell. The pigs rolled about a bit but nobody seemed to mind. We were greeted by the island's most important person, Chief Tom Numake. Chief Tom was big, even by the standards of the Melanesians, who are not small, and exuded a splendid awareness of his salience, political as well as personal.

Later, when we got to know him better, I naïvely asked him, 'What exactly are you chief of, Tom?'

He seemed to expand, threw his arm wide in a gesture which swept the horizon. 'I chief of *Tanna*,' he said. It was grand.

(What he actually said was something along the lines of 'Dispela emi nambawan blong Tanna', but no doubt you get the drift.)

Tom was our guide for the next few days and drove us around the island in a small, yellow Suzuki jeep. Two things are worthy of mention. Firstly, he showed us the temple of John Frum, of whom we had heard but about which nobody seemed to know much. Tanna, possibly because of its remoteness, had resisted the infestation of Christianity and now had a god of its own, John Frum. His temple was constructed of pandanus branches, as were most of the other edifices in the islands, and thus far not remarkable. What was remarkable was its decoration, for it was festooned, inside and out, with advertising materials and packaging from every variety of goods produced by Western, mainly American, consumerism. There were whisky bottles (empty) and cigarette packets (ditto), soap flake ads and a colour photograph of a yellow tractor. The central belief of the religion was that if you lived a good life and (importantly) were prepared to donate to the chapel, John Frum would answer your prayers and bring you goodies. If not in this life, certainly in the next. Since the donation of empty packets was acceptable and the return presumably to be in the form of full ones, the religion was popular.

The foundation myth relates that in 1942, as the American forces built up to what would become the battle for Guadalcanal, forward bases were established in the New Hebrides, though not in Tanna itself, where there was little flat ground to land on. One night a Dakota freighter, loaded with comestibles for the US troops, was forced to crash-land on Tanna, which it managed to do without loss of life. In the morning when the islanders came to view the scene, they were met by an airman who stepped out of the door of the wrecked aircraft saying, 'Hi guys. I'm John. From America.' He then handed out Hershey bars to the astonished islanders who understandably considered him divine. By the time the Hershey bars and whisky were finished, it was assumed that this was only a first coming and that, if the people behaved themselves, there would soon be a second. Not a bad religion at all, and mercifully free of metaphysics.

Our second and most important objective lay on the other side of the island and, though some twenty miles away, it was constantly in view. It isn't big, as volcanoes go, but these things are relative and compared with Tanna it looked very big indeed, with a little curl of smoke at the summit hinting at the fire in its belly. Chief Tom drove us to the foot but would go no further even though there was a rough track most of the way to the summit. It was plain that the presence of the mountain was in some way daunting to him for he treated it with respect and awe, much more of both than he had shown to John Frum. Dick and I were quite happy to hike to the summit, though we did regret having only sandals on our feet, for the lava was coarse stuff. Chief Tom bestowed plastic bottles of water upon us and said he would await us in the village nearby.

Viewed as a mountaineering ascent, it didn't amount to much, though I was more accustomed to mountains which – avalanches apart – stayed put. This one gave a little tremble every now and then. As we ascended, the trembles became more pronounced and accompanied by a low rumble. It was easy to understand why the local people believed that the thing was alive. When, after three hours, we came to the lip of the crater, we saw the cause of both shake and rumble. The crater was maybe half a mile across, its edge sharp and crumbly. The sides fell vertically for about two thousand feet and at the bottom were pools of molten lava, red and boiling. Every few minutes one or both of the pools would explode and throw its contents far into the air. When that happened, the whole mountain would shake and rumble.

The sensation of awe is not one which I have often experienced. Indeed, so unaccustomed was I to being awed that I had some doubt as to the meaning of the word. The time we spent on that mountain left me in no doubt at all. What struck me most was the feeling that I was in the presence of something to which human life was simply irrelevant; that here was a thing which had been since before the first creatures left the slime and would be long after the slime had dried and blown away.

We gave Chief Tom our last bottle of Society whisky. I expect that today, among the Twix wrappers and the Lucky Strike packets, it is to be found (empty), in the sanctum sanctorum of a John Frum cathedral in far-flung Tanna.

CHAPTER 15

The Lagonda and the Fall of Communism – Part 1

Since my motor car features regularly in this story, perhaps I ought to tell you about it. I bought it in 1974, when it was already thirty-seven years old, and I used it every day for the following twenty-five years, barring a few spells when it was off the road for repairs. I could never have been classed as an old-car enthusiast, for I didn't much care about old motors other than the one I happened to be driving. That this was a Lagonda 4.5 litre pillarless saloon was a matter of mere chance. I bought it for £500, drove it for about half a million miles and sold it for about twenty times what I paid for it, so it has to be classed as one of my better transactions.

I grew up in a society in which any reasonably well-informed boy could expect to understand how things worked and might, as I did, expect that when they stopped working, he could take them apart, find out what was amiss and fix them. This, I must admit, initially owed more to juvenile self-confidence than it did to an understanding of mechanisms, as Mrs Campbell's clock was witness. (Aged sixteen, I had volunteered to fix an heirloom grandfather clock belonging to the mother of one of my school friends. Having dropped the pendulum through the floor of the case, I retired, defeated and deeply embarrassed.) I think my arrogance was the product of a school curriculum which prized academic over practical subjects: irregular Latin verbs were important, the structure of our bit of the universe was not.

The fix-it mentality was applicable to most motor cars of that era and by the time I came to buy the Lagonda I had had several, none of which cost more than five pounds. All of them ran, though – some of them for years before they went to their next owner, the scrapper. In between, I kept them going by a variety of devices and in the process learned a bit about how they worked. I came to understand that the guys who made them were just as clever as the folk who knew about irregular verbs, if in a different way. For some years I was aided in my tinkering by a friend called Frank Levitt who, almost alone among my acquaintances at the time, was interested in things mechanical and appreciated their ingenuity. A Jew and a former delinquent from the slums of the Bronx, Frank had been saved from a life of crime by some Jesuits who, perceiving his for-midable intelligence, had thought to save him for Jesus. Under their care he matured to be a polemical atheist, which no doubt disappointed the fathers. He married a girl from Vassar, which created an interesting set of social problems in their homeland, but none in Edinburgh where Frank was studying philosophy. His main interest was philosophical logic, a discipline (if that's the right word) in which he would quickly lose me.

Frank had helped with the king-pins of a Ford Popular which had cost me four pounds but was disinclined to steer. Once it would go round corners it was a useful little machine and a capital cost of just under a pound a year seemed a modest price to pay for reliable transport. But when the Ford went to its long home (ten shillings from the scrap dealer) I was without transport, though I could occasionally borrow Duncan's van (Duncan of Denmill Farm, Chapter 1 and elsewhere). Duncan and I had a mutual friend, Murray, a dealer, in a small way, in antiques. In those days, before the great oil-induced inflation of the seventies, old things were of interest only to a small coterie of the antiquarian and a larger one of the poor. We met both criteria but, for such as we, Edinburgh was a good place to be, for all sorts of desirable artefacts could be acquired for next to nothing. And Murray was a past master at finding them.

One day I got a call from Duncan who said, 'Murray has found an old car in a barn in East Lothian. He says it's a Lagonda and the farmer doesn't want much for it.'

I told him to get lost because I had begun to set my sights a little higher, but of course we got into his van and drove out to East Lothian. The farmer was not at home but his wife directed us to a barn, in the doorway of which we could see the front end of the Lagonda. It was in surprisingly good condition, with no sign of rust. I bent over and lifted the bonnet by two handles. We looked at the engine, which was like nothing we had seen before. We tried the starboard side, but that was the exhaust and didn't enlighten us. Back to port, we gazed uncomprehendingly at a tangle of levers and copper pipes.

Wonderingly, I said to Duncan, 'I think that's a diesel engine.'

It was. It seems that in the 1930s the people at Gardner in Manchester had had the crazy idea that there might come a time when diesel engines would be suitable for motor cars, and they reckoned that they had the model for that future: their newly designed, ultra-modern LK series. A high-compression, high-speed (for the time) alloy-bodied lightweight, capable of being arranged with as many cylinders as you wanted. They bought two cars from Lagonda and put a six-cylinder machine in one and a four in the other. The latter was what Duncan and I were looking at. As far as Gardner were concerned, the venture was a failure. By 1950 they concluded that there would never be a market for diesel-engined cars and sold both the Lagondas, one of which was to come to me a quarter of a century later. The Second World War came along shortly after the engine was introduced, and versions of it were used in armoured cars, as well as the midget submarine which sank the *Bismarck*.

The Lagonda was a wonderful machine, provided you accepted it for what it was and didn't judge it against the performance of a modern motor car. By modern standards its acceleration was poor, its roadholding worse and its brakes tended to fade if you used them too much, which could be alarming. But it could do nearly a hundred miles an hour and would continue all day without apparent effort. Being a diesel, it was economical of fuel and the twenty-five-gallon tank, when supplemented by the spare fuel carried in one of the wheel arches, would allow it to travel a thousand miles between filling stations. It was seventeen feet long, more than half of that length being the bonnet, had two trumpet horns and headlamps the size of basketballs. Aft of the small saloon, its boot folded down to take a great trunk which was held in place by leather straps and buckles. It was painted silver, with the lower panels of bonnet and doors black, and it looked very classy.

There were however two unavoidable inconveniences: when it started it made a lot of white smoke, and when it ran it made a great deal of noise. The noise was mainly the pre-ignition knock which all diesels suffer from but in the Gardner it was really loud. There was really nothing to be done about either and I learned to live with them. On a few occasions I met an old-car snob who would look down his nose at what he thought was a petrol engine with wrecked big-end bearings. Not just a snob, an ignorant snob. Only once did I encounter a real expert.

Shift to Granton Harbour, middle pier, some time in the seventies. A fine morning and outside their workshop on the pier Walter and Watson Scott, marine and general engineers, are standing clad in dirty boiler suits, each with a mug of tea in hand, taking the morning air. I drive up in the Lagonda and draw to a halt before them. (It was the first time I had been there with the car.) I turn the engine off and when the din dies down and I get out, Walter addresses me.

'Is that a Gairdner?' he asks.

I nod.

'The splines on the timing shaft are worn,' he says.

Now I had recently had the engine rebuilt at enormous (by my standards) cost, mainly by Gardner themselves. They had replaced every part that was seriously worn and I had to all intents a new engine, save for a shaft which drove the injection pump. This shaft had shallow spiral grooves cut into it in which sat a dog, which could be moved fore and aft and thereby alter the timing of the pump relative to the crankshaft. A simple, ingenious and very expensive thing to make, for it required some fancy machining. I had decided, and Gardner, engineering perfectionists though they were, agreed, that the slight chatter which wear on the shaft occasioned, was tolerable. It was this chatter which Walter could hear above the din of the engine. Walter didn't think it was quite proper.

In the late 1960s I became one of those deplorable people who join political parties with a view to subverting them and persuading them to change some of their cherished policies. In my case the party was the Labour Party and the policies were to do with Edinburgh's transport system. The Town Council of Edinburgh had hired consultants to advise it how to cope with the congestion caused by the increasing number of vehicles using the roads. (This would be thought laughable today for by modern standards the town was half-empty – you could park anywhere in the city centre.) The Town Council decided that their consultants' advice was good (they had, after all, charged very large fees) and ought to be followed. So, in 1968, a plan was devised which would solve Edinburgh's transport problems. Motorways would be built which would facilitate the movement of traffic around the town centre: six lanes through Princes Street Gardens under the Castle, six lanes under Calton Hill and in a trench through the Canongate, an exchange up in the Pleasance and another six lanes in a deep cutting through the Meadows.

The Council miscalculated badly. There was an immediate outcry from all the people who cared about their city, and there were a lot more of those than the Council had realised. Hornets disturbed were friendly by comparison. One evening there was a meeting in my friend Chris Fyfe's top flat at No. 2 St Mary Street, at which a whole lot of angry citizens formed an association whose object was opposition to the motorways. For my part, I said that the ultimate aim must be to get hold of the political power in the Council and change its policies. There were only two parties, of which only the Labour Party seemed to hold any possibility of change. I joined it and, over the next few years, managed to get myself made chairman of a committee which recommended policy on planning and transport matters to the Party. Needless to say, our recommendations did not include a motorway through Princes Street Gardens. In 1974 there was a change to the structure of local government and the new (Labour-controlled) Lothian Regional Council adopted our strategic planning and transport policies. In those six years I naturally came in contact with a lot of professional town planners. One of the latter became a friend. His name was Bertold Hornung and he had come from Czechoslovakia, which was then part of the Soviet hegemony.

Berty Hornung had been born about 1925 and in his early teens was apprenticed to a cabinet maker in western Bohemia. By the outbreak of war he was in Prague where I think his family lived. In 1942 he was picked up by the Nazis (he was a Jew – there are a lot of them in this story for some reason) and put first in Theresienstadt concentration camp and later in Auschwitz. He was likely to have died in Auschwitz but the Nazis, finding he was a skilled woodworker, used him as slave labour building wooden barracks in eastern Germany. After the war, Berty studied architecture and then town planning in Prague, and looked set to be part of the socialist rebuilding of Czechoslovakia, having joined the Communist Party in the camps. I expect he was an awkward sod as a young man – he was awkward enough when I knew him – and he spoke out during one of the show trials at Prague University in the early 1950s. He was expelled from the Party and then fired from his job and that was, as far as the hierarchy was concerned, an end of him. But in those days, major architectural competitions were judged on the basis of closed submissions, and Berty kept winning such things, some of which had money prizes. They eventually threw him out of Prague but he was given a big job planning a new town in Eastern Slovakia. He pondered whether to tell the Party boss, assuming that the latter knew nothing about his past. As it turned out, the boss man didn't like the Czechs – he was a Slovak – and approved of most folk out of favour with his comrades in Prague.

When Alexander Dubček came to power in Prague in the mid-sixties, he scouted around for people who could help him build Socialism with a human face, and Berty was co-opted as head of planning for the rejuvenation of his favourite city, Prague. Berty had many stories about his time with Dubček, but my favourite is about the underground railway. Prague had an extensive urban railway system which had by then been running for a long time without repair and was in a very decrepit condition. It was underground and overground, and there were lots of tunnels and bridges. Because the Czechs, even under Communism, were pretty efficient and the Russians were not, a large national debt had grown up in the Czechs' favour. It was decided that this debt would be paid by Moscow providing Prague with a new urban railway. In 1967 this plan was put into effect and an entire kit of parts – rolling stock, rails, materials and personnel to install them – was sent from Russia to Prague.

The Soviet empire was run under a system known bizarrely as 'democratic centralism', which meant that decisions were taken in Moscow and everybody else did as they were told. Suggestions were unwelcome, and might prove dangerous to the person doing the suggesting, so the hierarchy was staffed mainly by yes-men and nobody thought to point out that where the Moscow underground is standard gauge, the Prague system was narrow gauge. The trains which had been sent were too big to go through the tunnels and too heavy to cross the bridges. At this point Berty got the unenviable job of running the show – but under a government which no longer deferred slavishly to the Kremlin.

I had been listening to this tale with astonishment.

'And what did you do, Berty?' I asked.

'Oh,' he said, 'I sent the lot back to Russia.'

'What exactly did that involve?' I asked incredulously.

'Well,' he smiled. 'It involved requisitioning railway trains and loading the stuff and the people on them and scheduling them on the railway system. I think twenty, maybe thirty train-loads in all.' He smiled wryly. 'It was hugely satisfying.'

Viewed purely as a career move it left something to be desired and a few months later, when the Red Army tanks rolled across the Czech border, Berty was on a list of collaborators destined for Siberia, or worse. It was a nightmarish situation, for the family had little money and most of that was not convertible into Western currency. Hannah, Berty's wife (whom he had met in Auschwitz), and their two daughters were far apart in the country and Berty described driving around frantically to collect them in time to catch the last plane out to Vienna. At Vienna airport a reception centre had been set up for Czech refugees. Each Western nation had a stand and was processing emergency visas.

'What decided you to come to Britain?' I asked.

He smiled. 'That's easy. The queue for the British stand was the shortest.'

Berty was fortunate that by then he had an international reputation as a town planner. He was asked to join the team of planners considering Edinburgh's transport problems, which he did, and the family came to live in a strange and alien city – but almost destitute, for they had been able to bring only what they could carry. Some friends found them a flat to rent in the West End and others contributed bits of furniture and they thought themselves very lucky.

One day, Berty and I were at a meeting and afterward he asked me back to the flat for coffee. The table on which he put our coffee was different from the rest of the furniture in both style and materials. Over our coffee I asked about it and Berty told me that he had made it out of old drawing boards. The timber – yellow pine – was not of the best but the execution was exquisite and Berty told me how he had begged and borrowed enough woodworking tools to enable him to employ his long-forgotten skills as a cabinet maker. But getting timber was a problem: not that there was a shortage, but he had little money and was without the network of contacts who might provide, and which I took for granted. I think I said something to the effect that I might be able to do something, and left.

At the risk of spinning this tale too far, I must tell you about my father. My dad was a docker in Grangemouth and he was a keen, if untalented, woodworker. Grangemouth at the time was the last port of call for some of the old imperial shipping lines which traded to the Far East and, having discharged most of their cargo in the port of London would, if there were consignments for Scotland, come up to Grangemouth. Some of the homebound cargo consisted of sawn timber which was sent ashore in a sling of wire rope. Sometimes a piece of wood would fall among the dunnage which occupied the bottom of the hold and was used for packing cargo. London dockers being what they were, there was no way of retrieving those pieces of wood and when the ship got to Grangemouth my old dad would climb down and forage among the dunnage. When he found timber worth having, he would call his friend the craneman, who would kindly send down a sling and haul the stuff ashore. Over the years a pile of sawn timber had accumulated at the end of one of the cargo sheds. Everyone knew it belonged to Jack Hills and that anyone who could make good use of it was welcome to help himself.

One day I took Berty down to meet my father and then we proceeded to the docks. The image of a child in a toyshop does not do justice to the sight of Berty among the timber, incredulous that anyone should have such stuff and that it was his for the taking. It was the start of a friendship which lasted until he died. In return, over the next few years, I was taught carpentry by a master. In particular, Berty showed me how to sharpen tools. He said he had spent the first six months of his apprenticeship in Bohemia doing nothing else. A chisel is sharp enough if you can shave a sliver of skin off the top of a finger without drawing blood.

Over the years we became close friends, though there were important matters on which we did not agree. I deplored his liking for the Bauhaus style; nor did I approve some of his planning ideas. But I recall his telling me how, in the future, there might be indoor shopping centres where people need not be cold or wet – the malls with which we are now so familiar. His status in his profession grew and he was asked to go to Jerusalem as part of a British Council team advising the Israeli government on the development of the city. When he was there, the Israelis offered him a top job if he would stay. Later, when over a drink in Edinburgh he told me of this, I asked,

'Why not? Surely for a Jewish town planner jobs don't come much more important than that.'

'Yes, Pip,' he said, 'but I wouldn't want to live there.'

'Why not?' I asked, astonished.

'Well,' he replied. 'It's not simple.' (I didn't expect it would be, but I was surprised by the reason.) 'It's this way,' he said, 'in Israel today there are no Jewish jokes.'

It was, I thought, a very Jewish joke.

We often spoke about his beloved Czechoslovakia and we planned that if ever the country were free, he would show me around his home town of Prague – and we would go in the Lagonda. One day, in the autumn of 1989, I called and in some excitement said, 'Berty, first Poland, now East Germany and Hungary. I think we should plan our trip.'

But I had caught him in one of his glooms: 'Alas, Pip, you must remember I am a convicted criminal in my native land.' (There had been a trial some time after 1968 and Berty had been consigned in absentia to Siberia.) 'I fear I can never go back.'

Recognising the symptoms, I apologised and rang off. About a month later I got a call.

'Pip, this trip to Prague, shall we make it April or May? We can go in the Lagonda and Hannah can fly and meet us there.'

I said April sounded fine, so the matter was decided. Except that in December Berty had a heart attack and had to call off, for there was no immediate prospect of his being fit for the trip. But by the early spring he was much better and we devised a plan whereby he and Hannah (who didn't want him out of her sight) would fly, and I would drive to Prague, where I would meet them.

CHAPTER 16

The Lagonda and the Fall of Communism – Part 2

The trip to Prague was planned for May 1990, so naturally it took pace in June. Since Berty would be going by air, I thought it would be good to have some company in the Lagonda and, in London visiting my sister, I mentioned this to Dick Pountain. The two had lived together for years, so Dick was part of the extended family. (He became part of the legal family when, after cohabiting with Marion for twenty-seven years, he finally asked her to marry him; clearly not a man to do things without due consideration.) Dick is a very smart guy who understands a lot of things I don't. He is from Derbyshire, whose folk rival the Scots for reticence and laconic observation, and surpass them in the matter of black puddings. He is an old biker, having owned some splendid machines and, having long ago been editor of a motorbike magazine, has experience of many more. He is also a renowned expert on computers and a sublime blues guitarist.

Dick thought a trip to Prague a fine scheme so on a day appointed he came to Edinburgh and the two of us put some stuff in the trunk and we set off. I had taken a few precautions:

a decent tool kit, some fence wire (useful for all sorts of repairs), a spare inner tube and a few tubes of epoxy resin. Also five gallons of oil in the spare fuel tank, for the Lagonda burnt a gallon of oil every thousand miles. I had filled the fuel tank, changed the engine oil, greased the wheel bearings and fettled all the steering joints. It was a fine morning and we were in high spirits. And, of course, I packed a case of Society whisky.

The run to Hull was unremarkable, as was the ferry crossing to Rotterdam. Then rolling up the Rhine just in time for Spargelfest: a celebration of the asparagus that was on the menu wherever we stopped. It was offered every time we did so, together with more wine than we thought it prudent to drink. The car was a great attraction and everyone wanted to know who we were and what we were up to. At the first hotel we stayed in, the folk in the bar found a word for us and what we were doing which appeared to give great satisfaction. We were, they concluded, engaged in *Schwagerurlauf* or 'brother-in-law spree', which was fine by us, though not to be legally exact for another fifteen years or so.

We left the Rhine just beyond Mainz and, passing Frankfurt, headed for the Czech border at Marktredwitz – after a short detour for Dick to visit Bayreuth, for he is a Wagner fan. The border itself was extraordinary. Externally it looked forbidding, as no doubt it was meant to, but among the guards there was a spirit of holiday. These were guys who had spent years obliged for their wages to behave like border guards in a John le Carré novel. And now everything was changed. We had been worried about duties on the dozen bottles of Society whisky we were carrying, but we were waved through without so much as a glance.

Just short of the border, on the German side, was an enormous truck stop and restaurant, its parking lot crowded by huge transcontinental lorries. Inside, the truckers were eating food of a sort then unknown in Britain, especially in transport caffs. We sat at a corner table and after a while noticed that we seemed to be of interest to a group of truckers, whose earnest discussions were accompanied by glances in our direction. A conclusion seemed to be reached and a delegation approached us. We couldn't imagine why we should be thus addressed, and were slightly concerned. We needn't have been. They asked, were we English? We nodded, or at least Dick did. Then came the demand, though not as we had apprehended: they had been looking at the car which was parked outside and was there any chance we might be so kind as to let them see the engine? We *were* so kind and when I lifted the bonnet, joy was unconfined, for a diesel engine was the last thing they expected. All of those guys drove diesels and some of them were diesel engineers. I had to explain about Gardners and what I said had to be translated. Then all their friends had to be called to witness such a wonderful thing. It was evident that one more thing would complete the general felicity, so, closely watched, I got into the saloon, pushed in the strangler, set the manual throttle control, retarded the fuel injection timing and pushed the start button. It fired first time, as I had known it would. The engine was of sufficient antiquity that it still had bits on the outside which went round and up and down when it was going, all of which were observed with great delight and speculated upon in several languages. A good goodbye to Germany and an introduction to what was to become the Czech republic.

We filled up with diesel just inside the border – our first since Hull – and headed for Carlsbad's faded splendour, where we spent the night. The following day took us to Prague, but on the way I had chronic trouble with the gear change. I had an idea of what the cause might be and on the outskirts of the city we stopped in a layby where I got out the toolkit and addressed the problem. The drive from the diesel was transmitted by way of a gearbox, which I think had been designed for a Mark VII Jaguar among other things, but the Gardner turned a lot slower than any Jaguar engine, so an overdrive box had been added. This, by a firm called Laycock, was an excellent device which was operated electrically from the cab and the solenoid was the cause of our trouble. I had just about reached it when there appeared a little man in a blue boiler suit. Where he came from was not apparent, and there seemed a possibility that he might be a Good Fairy, but he asked in excellent English if he could help. He said he had been in England during the Second World War, servicing Spitfires for the Free Czech Air Force. He did help. We removed the solenoid, cleaned and replaced it, and it gave no further trouble.

As we approached Prague's city centre it became apparent that something was going on. There were crowds of people in holiday mood and the nearer we got to the Old Town Square, the more old cars we saw, mostly Tatras and Skodas – Czechoslovakia had been one of the great cradles of the Industrial Revolution in Europe – and after all the drab years of Soviet domination, people had brought their treasures out of sheds and garages to join the great procession for democracy – for it was the day before the first free election, organised by Václav Havel's Civic Forum. There seemed to be no objection to our joining in the procession: indeed, it would have been hard to avoid it, so the Lagonda, by now somewhat muddy after driving across half of Europe and with its great trunk strapped on the back, became part of the movement for democracy.

I don't need to tell you that Civic Forum won by a landslide, and there was no shortage of drink taken. We met up with Berty, who had arranged for a friend's house to be made available for us to stay in, just a short walk from the Starometska, the town square (which of course isn't square). Dick met a chum of his, a journalist who was covering the election for the *Financial Times*, and he introduced us to the mostly young staff of the *Lidové noviny*, the Czech daily newspaper, who were all very excited and insisted we join them at concerts and parties in return for drives in the Lagonda, waving scarves and calling to their friends. The next few days are a bit hazy, though I do clearly recall one morning when I awoke and realised I had no idea where I had left the car. I think I have mentioned the fact that the doors didn't lock, so anyone might have taken it – if they were able to start it. But I needn't have worried: some younger members of Civic Forum found it some distance away, in a narrow one-way street, facing the wrong way.

A few days after the election, when everyone was more or less sober, a grand reception was held for Berty at which lots of people made speeches (in Czech, of course) and he was awarded a medal, and afterward we all had lunch in a wonderful art deco restaurant looking out over the city. Later, Dick and I hosted a tasting of the Society whiskies and an interpreter tried, I fear unsuccessfully, to explain why the whiskies were so much better than any the people had tasted before. It didn't really matter that the explanations failed, for most of the audience paid more attention to the spirit than they did to the words, or, you might say, to the spirit of the words.

For some reason that I don't recall, I had formed the idea that there might be good wines to be found in Southern Moravia. There are vast vineyards there, most of which grow the Müller Thurgau grape which, when made into wine, produces an alcoholic substitute for lemonade but not, as far as I know, wine of any distinction. However, thither we went and, over a week or two, sampled a lot of wine, all of which was pleasant enough but none amounting to a great discovery. Certainly nothing to compare for quality with the beers we had drunk in Prague and Pilsen. The towns were good, though, and the people hospitable: the latter mainly on account of the car which, appearing so soon after the announcement of freedom from Communism, seemed a harbinger of more interesting times.

It was another of those lost periods, dawdling through a summer landscape in Eastern Europe in a period when human affairs looked more promising than they have done for many a long day. Our only constraint of time was an invitation to a party. My chum, Jeannie, had had a relative who for some unknown reason had bequeathed Jeannie a little patch of woodland in Fife. At the end of June each year, Jeannie hosted an al fresco party in her wood, and I had been invited.

The car performed admirably on the return journey with but one exception. One day, when we were bowling happily along through hilly country, a bang and a horrible scraping sound announced that one of the supports of the silencer had given way. The silencer had parted from the exhaust pipe and fumes started to appear in the cabin. We stopped. I got out and crawled underneath, where I soon saw what was wrong. It was one of those jobs which would have taken five minutes with an arc welder but the last village we passed was ten miles back and there was absolutely no traffic on the road. Dick, looking on the bright side, pointed out that it was a lovely day and proceeded to open a bottle of the wine we had bought at our last stop. Sitting philosophically on the running board, we drank a glass or two.

I won't go into the detail – or not much of it. I hammered the two pipes together and fabricated a support out of the fence wire I carried in the toolkit. I mixed up a paste of epoxy resin and sand from the roadside, with which to plug the pipe joints and stabilise the bracket I had made. Then I had to clean the surfaces to which this stuff would be required to adhere. This was not easy: remember the motor was old and all its life it had been powered by a diesel engine – and no old diesel I ever met wouldn't leave oily deposits. We wiped the putatively mating surfaces with rags soaked in white wine, but that didn't suffice. Then I had a good idea: we still had a bottle of Ardbeg in the trunk. It was ferociously peaty and the Czechs didn't care much for it. It was also ferociously strong and its alcohol component was capable of dissolving any oil. The joins I made lasted all the way home and for a couple of years after. The trip through Bohemia, Saxony and Holland was uneventful. I dropped Dick in London and, driving through the night, arrived at Jeannie's wood (I thought) rather dramatically, for the car was very travel-stained and dirty, as was I.

'You're late,' Jeannie said. 'What kept you?'

CHAPTER 17

An Economist, an Artist and a Poet

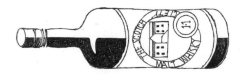

Economics has been described as the dismal science, which is unfair and untrue, for it is not necessarily dismal and it certainly is not a science. That said, it is not a discipline to which one turns for laughs, any more than dentistry, and in recent times it has been better-known for the destruction it has wrought in the hands of ideologues than for the good it has done. That this was not always the case, can be shown by the career of a visitor to the Society one afternoon. Kenneth Alexander was an excellent Scottish economist and a good guy to boot. For more than half a century his actions improved the lives of the people of Scotland, in many ways besides the merely economic.

Ken – he was formally Sir Kenneth, but nobody I ever met called him anything but Ken, which was an indication of the man's humanity – had been chairman of the Highlands and Islands Development Board for some years and it is difficult to think of any other individual who did more for the folk of the Highlands than Ken, an economist who cared about people. Though the Society at the time was not old and a continuing object of deep suspicion by the whisky industry, Ken had seen

155

what we were doing and liked what he saw. He brought with him a present when he came on his visit.

Among his many friends was an old highlander who, somewhere in the wilds of upper Glenlivet, had for many years been in possession of a small still, contrary to the provisions of the Excise Act of 1788. Also in contravention of the same act, the old chap had shamelessly been in the habit of using the still to distil his own whisky. But, feeling time weighing upon him, he had decided to make a present of the still to Kenneth. Now in those days the Excise made a practice of destroying any unlicensed still which came into their (or anyone else's) hands, and his friend gave it to Ken on condition that he do his utmost to ensure that it would not be destroyed or otherwise mutilated. As an occasional concession, the Revenue would allow a still to survive, but only if the owner was seen to have drilled holes in its bottom so that it couldn't be used again. (Presumably on the assumption that no prospective illicit distiller would have the wit to solder a few holes.) Ken promised there would be no holes. I don't know how he squared the Revenue who, armed with a tradition of centuries of bureaucratic obstruction, would probably have denied the Queen herself, but Ken managed it and for years it graced the head office of the HIDB.

This was Ken's present to the Society, a small recognition of his approval, but with one condition: that the still remain intact. I had no problem about giving such an assurance. I reckoned the simplest way was to say nothing and, if the Revenue discovered we had it, to make it disappear until times got better, as was the ancient tradition with whisky stills. It was lodged above the bar in the Members' Room and my only problem was discouraging Dougie, who was desperate to polish it. (I reckoned that a real illicit still ought to look the part and not like something out of a shop in the Lawnmarket.)

The still sat there for a year or so and I suppressed my urge to try it until one day we received another visitor. This was a gentleman by the name of Ralph Steadman who came by one afternoon in search of comfort, for he had just finished a book about whisky after arduous months of research, in which he had visited many distilleries and drunk many, many drams. I dropped by the bar and we fell into conversation. Ralph told me about his distillery visits and I told him about the Society. I think I may have mentioned the fake version of Scotland invented by the Victorians and adopted by the whisky industry for marketing inferior spirit. At the time my head was full of this stuff and I read Ralph some passages from Neil Gunn's *Whisky and Scotland* which was a diatribe against the distillers for depriving the Scots of their true national drink, i.e. malt whisky as opposed to blended. We drank a few drams and I adduced piece after piece of evidence for my thesis. I had an attentive audience. Ralph said that this was the first time he had heard anything of the sort and that it fitted exactly the suspicions which had been growing in his mind. In all his distillery visits the people could not have been more friendly and obliging – he was, after all, as famous an artist as he was a cartoonist and so worth a lot to the whisky industry in publicity – but he said that he had had a growing feeling that somehow he had been given the runaround; that there was a true story which he had not been getting. And this was it.

Ralph's reaction was not unusual, lots of people responded with indignation when I told the story, even though I was at pains to point out that, since none of us are responsible for the sins of our grandfathers, the present Scotch whisky industry was scarcely to blame. My view, and the policy of the Society, was that we should be happy that we had discovered the fact and, as a consequence of the discovery, a supply of peerless spirit. Also, we were able to occupy the moral high ground and have a lot of fun while doing so, not a common privilege.

Ralph didn't need a second telling. He could see all sorts

of possibilities and opportunities. It was about then that I told him about Ken Alexander and brought down the still to show him. He asked, could it be made to work? I said I saw no reason why not, practically speaking. The thing was intact, after all, and had not been altered since last it was used. We would need a worm, of course, and a worm tub, and a stand and some means of heating, but these were all details. And we would need a supply of wash, unless we were to make it ourselves. The night wore on until Dougie said he was needing his bed and suggested it was time we went to ours. Even this Ralph approved, for it was far from the deference customary in club bar stewards.

One thing remained to be done, he said. He was to send an email to his publisher, telling him to hold the publication of his book – *Still Life with Bottle* – so that he might write a final chapter, telling all he had learned that evening. In the morning the publisher told him to get lost and that the book was on its way to the printers, which was a pity.

A few days later I took a call. It was Ralph, saying he had had a good idea, and did I have a few minutes? Never one to resist good ideas, I said, of course. Ralph's plan was this: he was due to open that year's Cheltenham Arts Festival. How did I fancy running Ken's still as part of the opening ceremony? There would be lots of good publicity among the literate middle classes of southern England, who would surely be responsive to our story and appreciative of our whisky. Needless to say, I said I thought that a grand scheme. There were a few obstacles, of course, but I would see what I could do. The entire conversation took about a minute.

The main obstacle of course was the Law. If I were to do as Ralph suggested, it would be very public and we would have to have a distiller's licence and only the Excise could grant us one. HM Customs and Excise made the position perfectly clear: in no circumstances would they permit whisky to be distilled in a small still. I had phoned the head office, thinking that maybe a personal approach might be best.

I said, 'How about if we promise not to drink the whisky and just distil it for show? Maybe we could let folk smell it, but not drink it?'

The tones of outrage could be heard down the phone wire all the way from Perth; nobody had ever, in the last two hundred years, made such an outrageous suggestion. This was tradition and history talking, and it wasn't taking any nonsense. Or any prisoners, and I was warned of what would happen to me if I deviated in the slightest from the path of strict, to-the-letter righteousness. The sky would fall and I would be lucky to get a bottle-dungeon for a residence.

'And anyway,' said my interlocutor, 'where was this distillation to happen?'

'Cheltenham,' I said.

'Where's that?' asked my prospective incarcerator.

'Somewhere in southern England,' I replied.

'Oh,' he said. 'In that case, it's nothing to do with us anyway. You need to apply to the Excise in Cardiff. Here is their number.'

Cardiff, being unburdened by Scottish tradition in the matter of distilling, thought it a fine idea. I suggested that we get someone to give us some low wines and that we distil those to spirit. Cardiff said, fine.

'About duty on the spirit,' I said. 'How about if we only let people smell it but not taste it and then we pour the lot down the drain? It's an old still and it hasn't run for years. The stuff is going to taste pretty nasty anyway, so it's no loss if we dump it.'

'No problem,' said Cardiff. You could almost smell the lily of the valley down the line. I have always liked the Welsh, now it seemed they could sanctify even bureaucracy. A few days later a letter arrived. Couched in the friendliest terms, it gave me a personal licence to run a small still whenever I chose, subject to the conditions agreed. I think, though I can't be certain of this, that I was the first such licensee in over two hundred years.

Many years later, Perth discovered I had been distilling in Scotland with a small still.

'You can't do that,' they said.

I pointed out that I had a licence and quoted the reference number.

'That's all wrong,' they replied. 'Who gave you the licence?'

'Your Cardiff office,' I replied.

'Oh, that explains it,' said Mr Grumpy. 'They're English. They know nothing about whisky licensing.'

They weren't, they were Welsh, I'm pleased to say.

Ralph was delighted when I phoned with the news. It was agreed that the official opening of the festival would go ahead as planned, that he would make a speech and tell funny stories in the persona of W. C. Fields, while in the background I set the still to work. There remained a few problems, but none insuperable. I had told my friends up at Macallan of the plan and they were all for it – Macallan had been supportive of the Society from its earliest times. Given their whole attitude to the distillation and maturation of whisky, and the consequent excellence of their products, they were as much an indictment of bad historical practice as we were. They just didn't shout about it as we did. When they heard of the planned distillation, they offered to supply, gratis, a quantity of Macallan low wines which we might distil. Needless to say, we accepted gratefully.

As it stood, Ken's still was just that, a simple pot-still, and the ancillaries would be needed. The plumber's supplier furnished the material of the worm in the form of some copper pipe, which I bent into a worm round a dustbin and connected to the still head by a screw fitting from the same supplier. An hour with a welder knocked up a stand for the still out of mild steel, a camping gas stove provided a reasonably safe source of heat and an old hogshead cut in half a worm tub.

I loaded the lot into the back of the Lagonda and set off for Cheltenham.

I had never been to a literary festival before. It was much cheerier than I had expected and much more fun. There were of course a lot of books about, which was no bad thing, but none of the people seemed particularly literary, not the pain-in-the-arse sort of self-conscious literary I associated with Milne's Bar in Edinburgh. Ralph was in high spirits and dressed for the part. I set up the still to the left of his podium and went in search of water for the worm tub. Someone found me a hose pipe and a tap: only then did I realise that the worm tub was going to leak abominably, for I hadn't thought about sealing the hole where the worm left the tub. But I hadn't been around boats for much of my life to be stymied by a mere leak, and a few rags caulked the space around the pipe. I filled the still and fired up the gas stove.

The multitudes assembled, Ralph began his pitch as W. C. Fields. I had never seen Fields in the flesh, but Ralph's imitation was a close approximation to the films I had seen, save that he was, if anything, funnier. He had planned his intro to last (I think) half an hour. I had started some time before and by the time he was ten minutes into his routine, the wash in the still began to boil. I cut the heat back a bit, to a gentle simmer, and sat by the mouth of the worm with a can. The air was warm and quite still and, very gradually, the unmistakeable (to me) aroma of malt began to permeate the auditorium. I waited with the can for the first drips of spirit.

Ralph said afterward that the last ten minutes of his spiel were heavy going. Early on, he had told the people what I was doing. Gradually, the attention of the whole audience swivelled from the speaker to what was going on beneath him. Most of the people had little idea of what to expect, for you must remember that in those days whisky distillation was a mystery to most people. And for those who did have some knowledge, it wasn't easy to see the connection between pictures in books of shiny pot-stills and the Heath-Robinson apparatus beside the stage. But the gods were on our side: just as Ralph wound up, the first few drops came dripping from the copper into my can.

Later he announced that he had never been so completely upstaged, but he didn't care; it was fun and the people were happy. And they would all remember the grand opening of the festival. I was subsequently besieged. I explained time after time what was going on; I poured whisky into glasses which I gave to folk to sniff, telling them they mustn't on any account drink it, or I would be cast in chains. Some were satisfied with that; and I explained that it was an old, dirty still and the whisky would probably taste disgusting anyway, even though the wash came from the good and great Macallan. But of course some people wouldn't be satisfied and must taste the spirit, so in the haste of the moment I invented the only course which might satisfy the Revenue and maybe save me from gaol: I made them swear that if they did taste the whisky, they must promise not to swallow and spit it out into my bucket. After a few had tasted and confirmed that it did indeed taste foul, the pressure diminished.

Things got quieter, the crowds drifted away and I relaxed. A very old gentleman appeared. He walked with a cane and was elegantly attired in a cream linen suit, with a panama hat to match. At his side was a younger man, who seemed to be his minder. The old man asked a few questions which showed he understood what was happening. I gave him a glass of spirit and, having explained about the necessity of cask maturation, warned him to nose the spirit but not to taste it. This he did with consideration and evident intelligence. After a little while he thanked me very graciously, saying he had often read about whisky distilling but had never seen it in practice. He turned to his minder, who gave him a little Penguin paperback book and a pen. Scribbling in the book, the old gent presented it to me, asking that I would kindly accept it as a token of his appreciation.

When, later, I looked in the book, I saw that it was a book of poems. The name on the title page and the signature were the same, it was Laurie Lee.

PS. In the course of the changes that happened after I left the Society, Sir Kenneth's small still has disappeared from view. If anyone knows its whereabouts the management of the Society would be more than pleased to hear from them.

CHAPTER 18

Good Relations

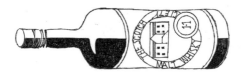

In the beginning the Scotch whisky industry simply ignored the Society. Small firms had come and gone over the two centuries in which Scotch whisky had risen from domestic production to become an important part of the Scottish economy. The big companies assumed, quite reasonably, that we would make a noise for a bit and then disappear, but they disapproved of trespassers and viewed us with irritation. They were very big and we were very, very small. That their attitude was compounded of annoyance and condescension bothered us not at all, for the very good reason that we knew nothing about it. In the early days Anne Dana was probably the closest of us all to the people in the industry, and since she was both clever and charming none of them were going to be less than kind to her. She was also streetwise and she found us a lot of good whisky.

As the years went by two things became apparent to the industry: we were still around and we were persuading people to buy whisky for which its distillers had been unable to perceive a market. We had a few moles, though not many, who would pass us information about what was going on. More than one account emerged from the secrecy of boardroom meetings in which an irritated chairman would ask his marketing director why our sales were rising and theirs were not, and why we were able to market spirit which had lain unsold in their warehouses for a generation. As you may imagine, this did not endear us to the marketing directors. The consequence was as predictable as it was understandable. In their resentment people would say, 'Well, they're not going to get *our* whisky,' and a ban on selling to us would be imposed. Happily for the Society, there was lots of fine whisky lying in the warehouses of brokers who had no such inhibitions, and supplies, though not plentiful, were sufficient.

Our approach was two-pronged. Anne would cultivate the people in the industry and I would persuade my friends in the press to write ecstatic praises of Society whiskies, especially in the supplements to the Sunday broadsheets. Names would be named, but only indirectly. When that happened, the marketing directors would be able to reply to their chairmen and say, 'Have you any idea what that mention in the *Sunday Express/Telegraph/Times/Observer/Mail* is worth to us as free advertising?' And the chairmen would slowly come around to the idea that maybe there was something to be said for us after all. Slowly, for the whisky industry moved with the speed of a termite mound, the idea grew that we might be doing some good, not just for ourselves but for the public perception of the entire Scotch whisky category. And we had lots of supporters among the more enterprising companies like Macallan and Glenmorangie, who had a lot of younger people in positions of influence.

We found that on the whole the bigger the company the harder it was to persuade them. And none proved more difficult to persuade than the biggest of them all: United Distillers. UD were the behemoths of the industry, owning more than half of all the distilleries and having enormous stocks of mature and maturing malt in warehouses all over the place. Fortunately for us their whiskies were so widely used in blending that lots of other companies had stocks of UD whiskies too, and we were able to obtain supplies from those stocks. But that left us without a long-term, reliable supply of some of the most important malts. It was obvious to us that in the long run we would have to lay down spirit in our own casks, but that required capital which we simply did not have, so we were dependent on the goodwill of the people who did have it.

The director of UD who mattered most in this was Turnbull Hutton, and we must have irritated him for he was said to have sworn we would get nothing from him. Since Turnbull was in command of the biggest stocks of malt on the planet, this was a problem. It was a bit of a standoff which I decided to do something about, though our Board were more inclined to wring their hands and try to be nice to Turnbull – which was a waste of time, for he was a very determined guy. (He was also a good guy, who just happened to be on the other side of the fence.)

It was about then that UD first brought out their Classic Malts. This was what is known in the trade as portfolio marketing: you create a brand identity under which you sell several related but different products. Because all of the products are covered by the one lot of advertising, it is economical and you don't end up competing with yourself, which is what happens if you own a lot of different whiskies and you say that each of them is the best. This was the first time it had been used to sell whisky – apart, of course, from the Society, which was the biggest portfolio of all, save that we didn't advertise. One day we had a visit from Andy Macmillan, who was in charge of the Classic Malts. I thought I might as well take the bull by the horns, so gave him a dram and said: 'You pinched that idea from us.' You can't get much more direct than that. He laughed.

'OK,' he said. 'But there's no copyright on good ideas, so there's nothing you can do about it.'

'How about acknowledging it, and selling us some of the other stuff you have stowed away?' I demanded.

'I'm afraid it's not my department,' he replied. 'You should try Turnbull.'

I knew what the response to that would be. Turnbull was sitting on huge quantities of perfectly divine malts for which UD had no use other than to mix them into one or other of their high-class blends. If UD was an oriental empire, Turnbull was one of its satraps and there was only one guy whom he would acknowledge as boss, the sultan himself. In this case the sultan was Lord Macfarlane (Norman Macfarlane as was), one of the good and the great, an industrialist and a philanthropist, and a very canny businessman. He had accepted the poisoned chalice of the chairmanship of Guinness at a time when his predecessor's actions in that capacity had caused him to be cast in gaol. Guinness had taken over UD shortly before and the cloud which hung over the whole enterprise could be dispelled only by someone of Macfarlane's undoubted probity. He was a High Tory, a peer of the realm, a Fellow of the Royal Society of Edinburgh and a Knight of the Thistle, so he need not defer to the Archangel Gabriel.

This was not the sort of company I normally moved in, so some careful thought was required if I were to gain access. To be honest, I forget just how it was managed, but managed it was and an appointment was made for me to wait on the great man at the headquarters of UD in Perth. The day appointed was in February, and it was cold and there was a lot of snow on the ground, so I considered taking the train but decided that was feeble – and besides, I had other things to do. I left myself plenty time to get to Perth, for, as I may have mentioned, the Lagonda didn't like ice or snow, and its heater was notional so appropriate clothing was required. It was only once I was on my way that it occurred to me that perhaps the gear appropriate to keeping frostbite at bay might not be the thing for the head of a great corporation, but by that time it was too late and my big boots and donkey jacket would just have to do.

I couldn't see any parking space that would take the Lagonda, so I left it outside the front door and went in. The lobby was big and, on the other side of an acre of marble, there appeared to be a receptionist. I could see her eyeing me and preparing to direct me to the nether regions, so I got in first: 'My name's Hills and I have an appointment to see Lord Macfarlane.' I could see she didn't like that but she was a pro and she urbanely asked me to wait.

I have to say that the old boy could not have been more affable if I *had* been the Archangel Gabriel, and we had coffee and scones, and both were very good. (I considered myself a connoisseur of scones.) And it also turned out he was a chum of Ken Alexander, who I suspect may have put in a good word for me. Anyway, we hit it off very well and I told him about the Society and our need for a tiny bit of his whisky and how much good we were doing for the name of Scotch whisky in places where it was needed. He said he would do what he could for us and I left with thanks. I heard later that Turnbull was none too pleased when the boss raised the subject, but the outcome was that though nobody would have said the dam had burst, cracks began to show and we got some peerless spirit which had not seen daylight for many a long year.

Some time, I think in the early nineties, I had another good idea. At least on first inspection it had all the characteristics of a good idea, i.e. it would be fun to do, it would get us some desirable publicity, it would make United Distillers happy, it would involve a fair amount of whisky drinking and it might even make me an honest shilling. Also, it necessitated some boat trips, which was always to be desired.

I had a friend called John Gibb, who was a journalist and

wrote pieces for the *Sunday Express*. Over a dram or two John had said he would like to do something about whisky and thought that if I could come up with something unusual, he could get the *Sunday Express* to do a big article in their magazine section, with pictures. This is the sort of thing that causes marketing directors to salivate, so I said I would see what I could do. At the time, the *Sunday Express* had a circulation of about five million. It happened that a few days later I was due to meet the chap who was in charge of marketing all the UD malts, so the proposal was opportune. Before I tell you how it worked out, I should tell you first about two boats.

One of the boats was mine: an Edwardian motor yacht called the *Kami no Michi*. She had been built by Dickies of Tarbert in 1911 for an officer in the Royal Navy who was on secondment to the Japanese. At the time the Japanese were building their imperial navy, and the British government approved of this because a strong Japanese navy would be a counterweight to the Russians in the Far East, and because the Japanese were buying lots of British guns and other armaments. (For a hundred years Russia had been perceived as the main threat to the British Empire and the government worked on the principle that my enemy's enemy is my friend. Not a hifalutin foreign policy principle, but it had worked pretty well for quite some time.) A number of British naval officers were seconded to Japan to show them how to run a proper navy, and one of them gave his new yacht a Japanese name. She was long and slim and very pretty, with an elegant bow and a canoe stern. She weighed about twenty-five tons and was a good sea boat, save that in a beam sea she rolled like a pig. She had been requisitioned by the Navy in 1914 and for the duration of the Great War she plied between Rosyth and Scapa Flow, carrying dispatches for the Grand Fleet. At the time of which we speak she was lying in Oban, which was handy for my plan.

The other boat was a puffer called *Auld Reekie*. Everyone who knows the west coast of Scotland knows what a puffer is, but in case you are not one of the elect, I will explain. A hundred years ago, communications with Scotland's western seaboard and the adjacent islands were mainly by sea, for the roads were very poor and only two railways served the whole of the west coast north of the Clyde, one to Oban and the other to Mallaig. What didn't go by rail had to go by boat – and this applied especially to bulk cargo such as malted barley for distilleries. The puffer was a small, ugly, bluff-bowed, steel-hulled cargo ship driven by a simple steam engine. It was flat-bottomed, so that it could be allowed to dry out on a sandy bottom and the cargo unloaded into a horse-drawn cart. By the early 1990s only two or three remained, and only one of those was still driven by its original steam engine. It belonged to two friends of mine, the brothers Derek and Brian Bathgate, and it was lying in Crinan Basin.

I proposed to the Bathgates that I should charter their vessel. They pointed out that its bottom needed plating and the engine hadn't run for years, objections which were ameliorated by the prospect of an appropriate charter fee. I said a run down to Lagavulin, possibly one to Talisker, but no more, and in good weather only, for my clients were averse to being drowned. An agreement was struck.

John liked the idea of an article about visits to three distilleries: Oban, Lagavulin and Talisker, the visiting to be done in two very classy old boats. Well, 'classy' in transatlantic parlance was probably inappropriate for the *Auld Reekie*, for she was a dirty old tub, but Brian had said they would wash her, if there was money in it; possibly even give her a lick of paint (a generous offer, I thought). 'Classic' she certainly was, in the significance attached to that term by people who think 'old' insufficiently complimentary, and the three distilleries we were to visit were among UD's Classic Malts, so the thing was a neat fit.

John was pretty sure he could get the *Express* to agree, provided it wasn't going to be too expensive. I said I thought a deal might be done and we went our separate ways. By the time we reconvened, John had had an enthusiastic OK from his editor and I had been to my man in UD, to whom I had put the proposition, with an estimate of cost. He didn't even haggle and agreed right away. I naturally wished I had asked for double, but rested content with a whopping great profit.

The trip was a big success. Both boats performed perfectly and I had an opportunity to experience a steam ship at close quarters. Two things struck me about the puffer. Firstly, how quiet the steam engine was. Accustomed as I was to the thunder of a diesel – any diesel, for they are all more or less noisy – I thought the steam engine made little more than a shuffling noise, with a bit of a hiss on top. Secondly, how much skill it required to operate the thing. I had naïvely assumed that to make a steam engine run, all you had to do was to keep the fire burning. In a sense that was true – but so much depended on the fire. It had to burn just perfectly if the ship were to make any serious way, and that, I can assure you, was no easy matter. The *Kami* was her usual obliging self.

We visited Oban, obviously, and then down to Islay and Lagavulin where the photographer took some daft shots of me in a small boat being rowed past the distillery by its manager, drinking whisky the while. For some reason the paper's picture editor liked that one and it made the whole of the centre spread in the *Sunday Express* magazine, the most prominent thing in the picture being the Lagavulin logo on the distillery. Needless to say, UD were delighted. Its value to them as advertising was probably worth many times what they paid me. Then the weather broke and the lads hired a charter plane to fly them up to Talisker, which saved us a trip. Turnbull was noticeably nicer to us after that, and some very fine malts were forthcoming.

CHAPTER 19

American Notes

About five years after we started the Society we were discovered by some Americans. They were malt whisky enthusiasts, at that time an uncommon species in the US. On my way back from Vanuatu I had spoken to some people in the wine trade in San Francisco and it appears they had passed on the information to their friends. It happened as follows. Before my trip to the Antipodes I had been in desultory correspondence with a lady in California called Okanta, who had said I should look her up were I to find myself on the coast. The crossing of the so-called Pacific had again been rough and I was disinclined for another flight immediately, so I called her from Los Angeles and she invited me to come and stay. I had the airline re-route me to New York from San Francisco, then I hired a car in LA and set off up the coastal highway, of which I had heard and read so much. The coast wasn't in the same class as the west coast of Harris, but I must admit the roads are rather better.

I allocated two days to the journey, for I wanted to visit Monterey, for literary reasons. It was the locus of *Cannery*

Row, a slim volume by Steinbeck which, read when young, was partly responsible for my preference for demotic company and my conviction that that is the source of all the best stories. I stayed the night in Carmel, an astonishing town built into a forest of pines: astonishing, in that they had contrived to build the town without cutting the trees down. Then, in the morning, to Monterey which was, as expected, a disappointment. (I think that's probably an oxymoron, but no matter.) San Francisco was even more astonishing than Carmel, with the steepest streets I have ever seen. Later, at a party, I asked, 'What do they do when it snows?' to general laughter, and my hostess gently explained: 'This is California; it never snows.'

It was soon after Christmas and appeared to be the party season in San Francisco. The people at the parties to which Okanta took me were mostly youngish, middle-class, college-educated and they liked to talk. Much of the conversation revolved around what I would have classed as religion but which the people mostly referred to by other names, none of which made much sense to me. And there appeared to be no limit to how long they could go on talking about it. Some years before I had had a passing interest in Mahayana Buddhism, I had a superficial acquaintance with the *I Ching* and a couple of philosophy degrees from Scottish universities, so many of the terms they used were familiar to me, though I had no high opinion of them. It wasn't difficult, given a rudimentary grasp of the vocabulary, to string together observations which they seemed to find an acceptable contribution to the conversation. But I soon began to find the conversations tedious, not least because there appeared to be a convention that nobody *argued* about anything. If what you said was couched in terms of spirituality in any of its many variants, it was OK, Man. A lot of the stuff was what came to be known as New Age and it was mostly drivel, and, for no apparent reason, the belief system often involved faith in the curative powers of crystalline minerals. There was lots of apocryphal and anecdotal support for this, but nothing that would stand up to scrutiny by a dim ten-year-old.

To relieve the tedium, I began, quite gently, to point out that some of what was being said was mere nonsense. (In fact, almost all of it was nonsense, but when in Rome . . .) This was thought first astonishing and later amusing. I took a high line in argument and used more than a few Anglo-Saxon adjectives and sundry vulgar terms whose meaning was often opaque to my listeners but conveyed the force of my scepticism. Plainly most of those people had never heard anyone laugh at their cherished beliefs, and then explain why they were funny. When asked for my alternative to the loopy religion, I would argue in favour of common sense and suggest that the spiritual element might be provided by good malt whisky. I was mostly making it up as I went along.

As the week went on, and the invitations to parties multiplied, my hostess pointed out that many of the people inviting her to parties were specifically asking if she would bring her Scotch friend along. It appeared that I had acquired a following and that a lot of people were taking what I said very seriously. Since most of what I said had been anything but serious in intent, this was worrying, and it appeared that I was in danger of acquiring acolytes. My reaction to this was first alarm and then compassion. Alarm at the thought of people thinking seriously about nonsense I had uttered for amusement, and compassion that there should be so many people desirous of believing something, but unable to find any satisfactory basis for belief other than a daft man who was having a bit of fun. It was therefore with some relief that I caught a plane for the East Coast some days later. I did, though, reflect as we passed over the Rockies that if ever I were in need of a way of making a living, I would go to 'Frisco and start a new religion. I *have* had such a need on several occasions but I'm afraid there are some things I won't do.

By the late eighties, malt whisky was becoming fashionable in North America. The fashion was part of a movement which, rejecting some of the more undesirable aspects of modern life, demanded more original, authentic sorts of food and drink, especially drink. It was a time when real ale was beginning to be in demand in the UK and, predictably ahead of the wave, folk in New York were establishing micro-breweries. Some people looked for similar qualities in distilled spirits and, unsurprisingly, found them in single malt whiskies. There wasn't much competition: vodka is just alcohol, gin the same with flavourings, rum virtually unknown, whiskey rough peasant liquor and the flavour of Bourbon the victim of its maturation. I'm not saying that none of those spirits are incapable of fine expression: merely that there was none of it around at the time. Brandy was long-established as an upmarket liquor but had been blended to appeal to the perceptions of the aged who could afford it. So malt whisky got a lot of attention.

Some of the malts available in the USA were very good indeed: Glenfarclas, Macallan, Glenmorangie and several others, but what they lacked was a narrative, a story to aid their perception. And what the Society had, above all else, was a story. This at least was apparent from the Americans who had made their way down to The Vaults in Leith. It was the story that guaranteed the authenticity and the people who, having heard the story, sampled our malts, needed little convincing. They all asked the same question: how can I get this stuff in the USA? When are you going to open a branch in New York or LA or Baltimore?

We could see that the market for the Society in the US must be huge. The problem was, how to get to it on the basis of our very slender capital. There were several government departments which were tasked with helping prospective exporters such as we, and we duly contacted them. They offered advice but little else, though to discover that we had to spend a lot of time filling in forms and going to interminable meetings, which appeared to be about something but weren't. Some things we did learn, though: that to get liquor into the US, we would have to jump through all sorts of hoops. It was then that we discovered why almost all the distillers chill-filtered their whiskies. This was because an unfiltered whisky left in a cold warehouse will throw a sediment, and sediments were unacceptable to the ferocious US Food & Drugs Administration. You can see why people smuggle narcotics; no doubt some of them do so because they are criminals and to do otherwise would damage their professional reputation, but I'm sure a lot of them are smugglers because they can't face the form-filling and attendant regulations.

It became apparent that we needed someone who knew his way through the system: an established importer of wines and spirits, but one who was prepared to represent a small and highly unorthodox whisky company. And he had to be someone who could see the necessity of the Society structure and not just use us as a supplier. And then we found Alan Shayne – or, more correctly, he found us. Alan, and his charming wife Maddie, owned Spirit Imports Inc., a small company which imported wines and spirits, and they were looking out for new opportunities. Alan paid us a visit, we showed him our premises and we laid on a tasting of some of our malts. We also explained the nature of the Society and how the value of membership was related to the ban on direct advertising. I was able to show him press cuttings which demonstrated the efficacy of this approach and he had no trouble seeing how our story would play in the American press. We had recently hosted a tasting for *Decanter* magazine and were able to show him the write-up, which was praise verging on adulation, and a tasting of whiskies for our

London members was scheduled, so we could show Alan how the thing worked. He didn't take much convincing, and I could see that someone like Alan (big, well-built, expansive in gesture and cheerful in demeanour, friendly and fluent), would make an ideal front man for the Society in the USA.

After that, things moved quickly. Alan invited us to meet him in New York and the following month a few of us did so. His company imported cigars as well as spirits – and in the US the two went naturally together. He invited us to an event entitled The Big Smoke (which had nothing to do with London or fog) at which mostly middle-aged, well-heeled New Yorkers sampled spirits and cigars together. I had reservations about the cigars for I maintained that nobody could discern the flavours of good whisky while smoking a cigar. I was a bit more assertive then than I am now and less appreciative of the human capacity for olfactory accommodation. If you can perceive the scent of violets in a Laphroaig, you can taste whisky through cigar smoke. Not that I would recommend the practice all the same, for the smell of someone else's cigar can be intolerable. Alan opened the Scotch Malt Whisky Society of America very shortly after, and it has attracted large numbers of American whisky drinkers ever since. The modus operandi is different from that in the UK, but not very. As far as I know, they continue to smoke cigars.

It quickly became apparent that there would be a lot of interest from the press. Alan knew just about everyone in the business, so we had no shortage of introductions: *New York Times*, *Wall Street Journal*, *Forbes*, *Wine & Spirit*, *Wine & Food*, and several others. All could see the quality of what we offered, so they needed little convincing about our story. Alan organised whisky tastings (with cigars) at venues across the US, from New York to Los Angeles. I attended a fair number and did my usual spiel, which went down very well. The notion that here was a small, independent company marketing the finest product of the great Scotch whisky industry was one that almost everyone could relate to. It was entrepreneurial capitalism in the service of superlative liquor: what could be better than that? None of the whisky drinkers seemed to set much store by therapeutic crystals.

I might mention that one of the venues that Alan arranged in New York was in the World Trade Centre. On the top floor of the South Tower was a restaurant called Windows on the World, where we hosted a whisky tasting. The view, from windows which stretched from floor to ceiling, was just amazing. After the event was over, I stood at the window, looking down over Lower Manhattan to the Statue of Liberty, talking to a New York lawyer whose office was in the same building, on the 55th floor. I said, looking past my feet to the plaza 1,200 feet below, 'It's amazing, but I wouldn't like to be here if some terrorist detonated a bomb.'

'You wouldn't have anything to worry about,' he replied reassuringly. 'There was a bomb in the basement last year and I didn't even hear it. The building is indestructible.'

I sometimes wonder what happened to him.

Over the following few years I made several visits to the US, travelling with Alan to many of the principal cities. The venues were without exception swanky, a transatlantic term for which there is no exact equivalent in English, denoting luxury, but without the connotation of social status which generally goes with luxury in Europe. I have no problem with this, save that the places were eminently forgettable. Perhaps the fact that all the hotels were owned and run by giant corporations had something to do with it. Giant corporations are not in my experience the natural venues for what I would call fun, save in the gross and dismal sense of fun that you would find in a theme park or a whorehouse.

Of all the places, Florida stands out in the memory. I blew into Miami one night, literally, on the tail of what they call a tropical storm, which is one notch down from a hurricane (I should estimate Beaufort Wind Scale ten or eleven). The atmosphere was akin to that of a Turkish bath, only wetter. Palm trees were touching their toes and the entrance to the hotel looked like a disaster movie. From Alan's demeanour this was plainly not unusual and the tasting of whiskies went ahead as though nothing was happening. I had to admire their sangfroid, for none of the guests seemed in the least perturbed.

The next morning Alan took me – by road, among blown-over trees and battered buildings – to visit one of his cigar suppliers in downtown Miami. The premises were emphatically not swanky; anything less swanky it would be hard to imagine, for they were a collection of down-at-heel low white buildings in the middle of a part of town which, though it would not have been classed as a slum, was certainly not affluent. Alan assured me that this firm supplied some the finest cigars in the world and that they were all hand-rolled and correspond-ingly expensive. He was a little coy about the origin of the tobacco leaf, though it was plain enough that it was Cuba – and therefore of doubtful legality. The people were delightful, both men and women, who were indeed rolling cigars by hand. Everyone was smoking. They offered me one, and I was sorry to decline, blaming my asthma. They were sympathetic; since in their world tobacco was the greatest good, it followed that my inability to smoke it was deserving of great sympathy. I think to console me, one fine lady produced a bottle of rum and poured me a glass of an amber liquid. Since the rum was presumably Cuban as well, I was happy to accept. It was lovely, and I said so, in the rudimentary Spanish I had learned from my daughter. I knew before I tasted that it would be good stuff, for it was not the first time I had drunk Cuban rum.

About twenty years before, in that short time in my life when I had a regular job, I had had occasion to go to London on business. I lodged with my sister who at the time lived with

Dick Morton, whom I have previously mentioned. Dick had been a friend of various Cuban revolutionaries and had spent some time in post-revolution Cuba, in his capacity as geneticist and expert pig-breeder. The aim was to improve the ability of the small, runty Cuban pigs to convert food waste into fat and protein by cross-breeding them with pigs from Wiltshire, so that they might become big, fat pigs like their ancestors – without losing the natural immunity to disease possessed by the local breed. As far as I know, it was a success.

They made me welcome as usual and told me that there was to be a party at the Cuban Embassy that evening, and of course I would have to come. I'm not sure what I expected of the Cuban Embassy: red flags, at least. The reality in West London was disappointing, for it was all very formal. I didn't have a lot of experience of foreign-embassy parties, but I reckoned this was probably in no way exceptional. Certainly the proceedings were pretty dull. There was champagne to start with, then a few speeches, a buffet supper and chat and cocktails. The only thing that attracted my notice were the big guys standing around not talking to anyone. They were very big and some of them were very black. All wore smart suits with double-breasted jackets, which showed slightly asymmetrical bulges near the left armpit. These guys were carrying weapons. Later, Dick told me that for years after the revolution, Cubans were in serious danger of assassination by the CIA, hence the routine arming of embassy staff. And, he said, those guys knew how to use their guns, for most of them had been with Castro in the Sierra Madre.

The cocktails appeared to be based on gin, which surprised me since I had assumed that they would use Cuba's excellent rum. But all the same, together with the rest of the party, I knocked back a few and we all got well-oiled. I don't recall the exact sequence, but at some point I seemed to hear myself saying, rather loudly, that I didn't expect bloody gin at a Cuban

Embassy party and where was the rum? Then I was picked up bodily by two of the bears. I thought that at the least I was going to be thrown out, at worst incarcerated in a cellar and sent to Siberia in a diplomatic bag. But no. One of the bears did the last thing I expected, he kissed me on the forehead before passing me to his colleague who gave me a hug. Then lots of bottles appeared and people began joyously pouring huge shots of rum into the cocktail glasses. It seemed that after the revolution the embassies were all staffed by comrades from the Sierra who had no experience of such things, but were doing their best to run an embassy properly and not appear to foreign governments as a bunch of hicks. And this involved making cocktails based on gin, and not their beloved rum. It seems I had been the first to call for rum in the post-revolution history of the embassy. The rest of the evening is a blur, save for when I went to the cloakroom to get my coat. The coat was rather splendid; heavy, of fawn melton, with big pockets and a hood. It had been an admiral's greatcoat; this I know because it had been bought second-hand in the Lifeboat charity shop along with a deceased naval officer's uniform: the rings on the jacket sleeves showed him to have been an admiral. As I say, the coat was heavy, and seemed more than usually so when I put it on. I put this perception down to my state of inebriation. It wasn't until we got into the taxi that I realised that in each deep pocket there was a bottle of rum, a present from the chaps with the shoulder holsters.

Chapter 20

American Papers

Alan's cigar smokers proved a fruitful foundation for the American venture and a great many of them signed up for Society membership. The smokers metamorphosed effortlessly into whisky tastings and all was sweetness and light, though the atmosphere could be a trifle opaque. Back at The Vaults we would occasionally experience a bit of friction, as when an American member, visiting, had to be asked not to smoke, for we had a no-smoking policy long before the legislation. He complied, but ungraciously, and muttered about 'Commies' for the rest of his stay. But most of our transatlantic members recognised that customs differ and put up with the deprivation for the sake of the whisky and the atmosphere. They all liked the place.

I had done little about publicity after the first visit, reckoning that, given the reception we had received from the press in the US, it wouldn't be long before we heard from writers hungry for a new story, for novelty is at a premium in the food and drinks business. I had a call one day from a person who announced himself to be Paul Levy; that he wrote for the *Wall Street Journal* and might he pay us a visit? Naturally I said yes, and a meeting was arranged. When we met, I gave him the usual spiel. He had evidently read the stuff about us in the British papers and I could see he was sceptical. Nonetheless, he apparently thought there was at least a chance that we might be the real thing and, after more discussions, we arranged that he and a photographer would pay us a visit in Leith. Thereafter I would take him round a few distilleries and, if he were satisfied, he would write a piece about us for the *Journal*.

He was plainly in a different league from your average journo. For a start, he was an intellectual and evidently the recipient of an expensive education. He is the only member of his profession I have met who, in discussing the origins of a name, would use the International Phonetic Alphabet to make his point. What he wanted was to be convinced that we were the real McCoy and not just a clever front for a run-of-the-mill whisky. I thought the best course was just to take him around and let him judge for himself. So we planned a jaunt: he and the photographer would come to Edinburgh and spend a day or two with us; then I would drive the three of us around the Highlands, we would visit a few distilleries, and he would come back for a final dinner in Edinburgh.

He liked The Vaults and what I told him of its past. He clearly knew enough history to understand what I was telling him and to be able to check that it was true. I gave some thought to where I should take him for dinner. Then as now, there was any number of smart restaurants in Edinburgh and a few in Leith. But those, I thought, would cut no ice. So I decided to take him for a meal at Khushi's Indian Restaurant. Khushi's is one of those interesting Edinburgh institutions which rarely feature in the tour guides. It serves Punjabi food and it is the oldest Indian restaurant in Scotland, having been established in 1947 to cater for students from the Indian subcontinent who came to Edinburgh to study medicine. It was originally in Lothian Street just by the Medical Faculty where, together with the Crown Inn and the Lothian Billiard Hall, it provided all that a medical student might require in the way of recreation. When I first ate there, Mrs Khushi did all the cooking in great, steaming cauldrons, and the Khushi children, in their school blazers, would do their homework at one of the tables in the late afternoon. The restaurant has no liquor licence but if you want beer, you may bring it from the pub across the road. As an accompaniment to curry, I preferred Mrs K's lassi.

When the university, in its progress of institutional aggrandisement, knocked down Lothian Street, the restaurant moved to Drummond Street just down the road, where it remains to this day. The tables are in booths with a bench seat either side. There are no tablecloths. After you have eaten, someone comes along with a cloth and wipes the table. You order your meal at the till and when it is ready, a man brings it to your table. Since all the food has been ready for hours, the process takes less than a minute. Despite the proletarian ambience, I knew how good the food was. Paul said afterward that Khushi's marked the beginning of his conversion.

I had arranged that the following day I would take the two of them to Speyside and said I would provide the transport. I think that when I turned up in the Lagonda they were a trifle surprised, but not unhappy. I loaded up their gear, seated them in the back seat and settled the black bear rug around them, explaining that it would be cold. It was: a fine, clear day in early April, roads free of snow, but very cold. It got colder as we climbed into the Grampians, but stayed clear. Our first stop was a little north of Aviemore; I braked sharply and pulled to a halt.

Paul asked 'What's up?'

I said, 'Just a moment,' and got out of the car. I ran back

down the road for a hundred yards and returned, holding by the ears a big mountain hare. Its fur was still in winter white and it wasn't long dead.

'What are you going to do with that?' Paul asked.

'I'm not sure,' I replied. 'But it's too good to waste.' And I put it with the luggage in the trunk.

We visited a distillery, I think Tomatin, and stayed in a hotel overnight, none of it memorable. The next morning we headed down the A96 toward Glenfarclas. There are some nasty twisty bits of road on the A96 and just past one of them I stopped again. This time I came back with a brace of pheasants which, still warm, had evidently been killed by the vehicle in front.

'More roadkill?' asked Paul.

'Yes,' I said. Then I had an inspiration, 'When we get home, you can come to my house and I'll make you a roadkill stew.'

The visits to Glenfarclas and Macallan went well and the attitudes and responses of the people at the distilleries dispelled any suspicion Paul might have been harbouring as to the authenticity of what the Society was doing. We then headed back to Edinburgh, which we got to very late.

The next day I went to the butcher and bought some pork belly, then met Paul and his colleague for lunch. We arranged that they would come round to the house that evening. I skinned both hare and pheasants and put the hare on to cook. (It would take a lot longer than the pheasants.) I chopped and fried the belly pork, some onions, garlic, a few carrots and a couple of sticks of celery which I added to the hare, together with a bottle of rather good red wine and some mushrooms which I found in the fridge. When I judged the time was right, I added the pheasants and made some parsley dumplings. It was no great shakes as cuisine but it all worked perfectly. Paul said afterward that what finally dispelled his suspicions of bullshit was the roadkill stew. He wrote a piece to which the *Wall Street Journal* devoted nearly a whole page. Alan reported a flood of requests from people who had read Paul's piece and would like particulars of the Society.

The personalised distillery tour appeared to be the most effective way of securing press coverage in the US. That was fine by me, and besides, given the right company, it could be fun. The only problem was that most of the people we wanted to write about us had already had distillery tours on other occasions. They understandably thought that from the outsider's point of view there wasn't a huge difference between one distillery and another, and consequently found the tours a trifle boring. I noticed that what attracted their attention was generally something other than the distilleries.

Paul Pacult was no exception. Paul is widely recognised in the US as an expert on distilled spirits and his *Spirit Journal* is very influential. He paid us a visit, as disposed to be sceptical as his namesake above, but convinced of the quality of the whisky as soon as he had inspected a few. And he knew enough about whisky maturation to know that our story was perfectly accurate. I took him on the predictable tour, with the odd sideshow of whatever I thought might please or interest him. I had had to explain that in Scotland there was little indigenous tradition of gastronomy to parallel the concern for quality in whisky. (There may be now, but there wasn't then. Even things as quintessentially Scottish as scones were hard to find at any level of quality. On my journeys around the country I used to go looking for them. I remember there was a post office near Arrochar where really good scones could be found, and of course the distillery manager's wife at Ardbeg made scones of surpassing excellence. But they weren't common.)

One place I knew where traditional Scotch baking could be found which had not suffered the decline in quality which marked the twentieth century was a remarkable restaurant called the But'n'Ben at Auchmithie, north of Arbroath. Auchmithie is one of those east coast fishing villages which is perched on the edge of a cliff. The building is a row of low cottages, each of which would originally have had two rooms: an outer and an inner, or but and ben in Scots parlance. The restaurant itself is run by splendid ladies of a certain age and an appearance of comfortable opulence, who both cook and serve seafood and cakes. It sounds an odd combination, but it works (and of course, they are rarely served together). The seafood is all fresh and local, for the crabs and lobsters come from the sea at the door and the smoked fish from Arbroath, just a few miles down the coast. The cream and the grains come from the Angus hinterland, some of the finest farming country in the northern hemisphere.

I asked the ladies to give Paul some Cullen skink. This is a fish soup made from lightly smoked fish (mainly haddock), potatoes, onions and cream. Paul declared it the best seafood he had ever eaten, which for someone of his experience, is praise indeed. The *Spirit Journal* published a complimentary piece about our whiskies and Alan was pleased. I suspect we owed a lot to the Cullen skink.

For a time there was no shortage of free advertising in the form of gushing journalism in the US. Alan was aware of its value, though I suspect some of our Board members were not, mainly because they knew little about the publications in which it appeared. This was not the case, though, with *Playboy* magazine, which carried a five-page essay by David Mamet about his visit to the Society. That is to say, they knew about *Playboy*, though perhaps not about David Mamet, for a Pulitzer Prize-winning author, playwright, screenwriter, film director and producer was a bit beyond their ken. I was a bit sniffy about *Playboy*, regarding it as a magazine for men who would rather contemplate sex than engage in it, and thinking that those were not necessarily the sort of folk I wanted to attract to the Society. But Alan had no sort of doubt.

He once asked me, 'Have you any idea what five pages of editorial in *Playboy* is worth?'

I predictably said, 'No, how much?'

But even Alan had no idea, though he was happy to profit by it.

David had married the daughter of a Scottish friend of my then wife, Leslie, who is a film producer. Leslie's partner in the film business, Trevor, had told her that David was coming to visit and asked her what on earth he should do with him. She had suggested the Society, which, since David liked distilled liquors, was a natural choice. I volunteered to take him down to The Vaults and give him a few drams, thinking that would be the end of it. As it happened, we had two meetings of the Tasting Committee scheduled for the week he would be in Edinburgh, so I suggested to the members of the Committee that we ask him to sit in. They agreed. This largely solved Trevor's problem.

The Tasting Committee at the time was in one of its better phases and we had some bright sparks around the table. David Daiches was one, and each of the Davids had read some of the other's work, and liked it, so there was an immediate rapport. That aside, they got on well and had a lot in common. David M. responded to the others in the team and recognised that he was in a position in which he rarely found himself, that of an amateur in a group of professionals. And the collegiate atmosphere of chaps having a good time with strong drink appealed to him.

The whiskies were good, well up to standard. David (Mamet, not Daiches) didn't know a lot about Scotch whisky other than the view then current in the USA, which was formed around blends, so the quality of the stuff we tasted came as a pleasant surprise. He was initially reluctant to spit it out, until he had a look at the labels on the bottles and saw the alcoholic strength of the whiskies we were tasting. I had explained the rationale of the Society to him that morning over coffee and in the course of the tasting we filled in the gaps. It was, as you know, an astonishing story and David's response was the familiar one, of surprise that any industry, possessed of such peerless spirit, should have been unable to perceive a market for it and have concealed its excellence beneath such inferior stuff.

So, one of the Western world's leading intellectuals wrote about us in one of the Western world's leading girlie magazines. We were happy about that, even if I was sniffy.

Forbes magazine came later. On one of my early trips to the US, Alan had introduced me to some of the *Forbes* people, who had attended some of our New York whisky tastings. I liked the people a lot: they were, without exception, sharp, lively and well-informed. Indeed, they were well-informed about a host of things I knew nothing about, but they seemed keen to learn about some of the things I did know a bit about, which made me well-disposed toward them. They were also knowledgeable about spirits generally and about Scotch in particular, and our approach to whisky fitted well with the very up-market profile which the magazine maintained. It was arranged that Alan would bring me to the *Forbes* building for a chat about what we might do together.

For those who don't know it, I should explain about *Forbes*. It is a magazine which caters for the tastes and interests of the rich, mainly in the USA but also around the world. It does so with little of the vulgarity which people like me generally associate with extreme wealth, for it aims at the rich and the aspirant rich who would like to be thought cultured as well as wealthy. That said, it is unashamed of its customer base and unblushingly announces itself as a bastion of capitalism, which I find rather appealing in its frankness. The magazine is sold by subscription only: you can't buy it on a street-corner newsstand, which keeps it away from hoi polloi. The articles in the magazine, which is published bi-weekly, are predictably about money, business, politics, technology, science and law, as well as those topics to do with something called lifestyle. (As I understand the term, 'lifestyle' refers to a set of ideals and aspirations to be adopted by people who have none of their own but have a lot of money and think they ought to be seen to have some.) Some time before we came on the scene, the management had decided to corral the lifestyle stuff into a separate pull-out section to be called *Forbes FYI*. (For those who don't know, FYI stands for 'For Your Information', i.e. information about how you should live as a rich person.)

Some time before going to *Forbes*, I had had lunch with my friend, the historian Angus Calder (son of Ritchie, who appeared in Chapter 2). I had been to the US once or twice and was intrigued by that most interesting society, especially as regards its relation to Scotland – for in the early days, the Scots had made up a large part of the emigration from the British Isles to the American colonies. I had some questions about ethnic minorities and it was the sort of thing that Angus would know about.

'Why,' I asked Angus, 'is there no Scottish ethnic minority in the USA? Italians and Poles and Irish and Hispanics are all recognised as identifiable ethnic minorities, but not Scots. There are lots of parades and gatherings at which Americans play at being Scots by dressing up in funny clothes, but there is no sense of their being an ethnic minority.'

Angus laughed. 'That's easy,' he said. 'I thought you were going to ask me something difficult. It's because they form an integral part of the dominant social class. They were there early, they had a lot of social cohesion so they helped each other; and Presbyterianism combines well with capitalism, so they made a lot of money. There aren't enough poor people of Scottish ancestry in the US to form an appreciable ethnic minority.'

(This wasn't quite true – but the poor people of Scots descent tend to be dispersed in poor parts of the country rather than in the cities.)

Forbes is an old Aberdeenshire name. The family established their publishing business in the early years of the twentieth century and it prospered greatly. The business is still owned and managed by the descendants of the founder. Their offices occupy an entire city block on New York's lower Third Avenue and are, given the prominence of the magazine, fairly low-key. After a couple of visits I became intrigued by what I learned about the building, for it appeared that in addition to being the head office of the business, the building also housed a museum. It is a personal, family museum, containing stuff which the Forbes family acquired over the years and presumably didn't know what to do with, but didn't want to part with either. (A predicament with which many of us are familiar, but on a much smaller scale.) There are some spectacular children's toys of a sort that nobody in his right mind would let a mere child play with, but what I wanted to see, and was eventually allowed a glimpse of, was the Fabergé. As you know, Fabergé was a leading Parisian jeweller at the end of the nineteenth century, who made toys and trinkets for the crowned heads of Europe. Some of those crowns sat on the heads of the Romanoffs, Emperors of All the Russias – until, of course, the Bolsheviks shot them. It seems that the Forbes family had for generations been buying up any ex-Romanoff jewellery which came on the market and had amassed a perfectly spectacular collection. I would have liked a longer look, but I had other priorities.

It was decided that *Forbes FYI* would do a feature about the Scotch Malt Whisky Society. Characteristically, no expense would be spared. The piece would be run by Ray Healey and Duncan Christy and the latter would accompany us on some of our tastings tours of US cities. In addition, a team from *Forbes* would visit Scotland and I would guide them round a few distilleries. Accustomed as I was to the parsimony of the British press, this was welcome news. It was particularly welcome because Duncan and I, though from very different cultures, agreed on most things – and we tested the accord on many occasions, for we talked constantly.

Duncan is to my mind the best sort of American – and you should bear in mind the fact that I like the US a lot and get along well with her citizens. He is slight of build, dapper in the sort of understated way that we think of as characteristically English – literate and literary, enquiring and fun. He became my guide to the foreign country that is the United States, and I his to Scotland. I can give two examples.

Alan had set up a whisky tasting in the usual swanky hotel somewhere in a place near Los Angeles called Beverly Hills. It was well-attended by well-heeled people, which was good for Alan's business and, incidentally, ours. I was, as usual, presented as the founder of the Society and had to be affable to a whole lot of people I didn't know and with whom I had little in common. But that was no hardship for, as I have said, I like Americans. But one encounter disturbed me. It was with a little, elderly woman, obviously rich from the gold with which she was hung. What was disturbing was her face: the skin was drawn so tightly over the bone of her skull that she looked like a death's head. A short while later, Duncan and I found ourselves on a balcony, a little secluded, and I turned to him and said, 'Dear Lord, Duncan, what was that?'

'That, my dear chap,' he replied – he was occasionally given to using very English phrases – 'that is the result of four facelifts.'

The *Forbes* gang came to Scotland and it was decided that they would visit Islay, with me as *gauleiter*. We did the round of distilleries and drank a lot of whisky – the distillery owners, being well-appraised of the importance of *Forbes* magazine, were more than obliging. The trouble with a lot of the stuff that people tell you about distilling and maturing is that it is much of a muchness, and anyone who isn't a dyed-in-the-wool whisky buff will soon tire of it. The *Forbes* people did and, though they went through the motions, I could see that their attention wandered. To relieve the tedium, I pointed out some of the wonderful Celtic crosses with which the island is dotted and gave a potted history of the early Celtic Church in Scotland. This they found interesting and, having procured some guidebooks, settled down to photograph a lot of the stones. I soon found myself answering more questions about the latter than about the distilleries, despite my disclaiming anything other than an amateur knowledge of them.

There is one tall bluestone cross which is very elegant and very beautiful, and, one evening in the pub, Duncan put me to the test, asking me what date I would put on it. I had no idea but I was aware that the psychology of the visit had developed in such a way that my reply was somehow critical to their belief in the whole of the story – of the whisky, the Society and all. I said I had no direct knowledge of the stone, never having seen it before, or having read about it, so, as usual, I made it up as I went along. I reasoned that the stone was too well-preserved to be fifth or sixth century, and too delicate, for the early crosses are massive. On the other hand, it was too antique in appearance to be later than medieval. I worked from the early and from the late, eliminating – as best I could – possible eras, and eventually guessed at the fifteenth century. I was right, according to the most authoritative of their guidebooks. By association, it followed that everything I had told them up until then was right too. The article appeared in *Forbes FYI*, with lots of pictures. Alan was delighted, as were the distillery owners, and I breathed a sigh of relief.

Apropos the Fabergé jewels, we had a meeting at *Forbes* on Third Avenue after the trip to Scotland to finalise the details of the magazine piece. Alan was in attendance, as were Ray,

Duncan and, to my surprise, Bob Forbes himself, who was in overall charge. I had flown over for the meeting and had asked Maggie to accompany me. I had told her about the Fabergé and said I would ask if she might see it. I did: charm and beauty succeeded where I might not have, for Bob said to Ray, 'You guys don't really need me at this meeting, do you?'

Typically, Ray replied, 'You're the boss, Bob. You decide.'

Bob said, 'In that case, come with me, my dear,' and whisked Maggie off for a private guided tour of the finest collection of the works of one of the world's great jewellers.

The relationships among the people in *Forbes* magazine interested me. There was an ease of address among them which I don't think you would have found on this side of the Atlantic. As Ray had said, Bob was the boss, and the man who paid their salaries, besides being a member of one of the richest families in the world. There was nevertheless a social ease which I found pleasing. I was reminded of eighteenth-century accounts of the attitudes of clansmen in relation to their chiefs: the former addressed the latter with the perfect ease born of an assumption of common ancestry and social equality, without ever questioning the chief's authority.

One final word about that American trip. When my sister discovered that Maggie was going with me to New York, she immediately said, 'Dick and I will come too. We can all go and stay in Felix's house in Connecticut.' (Felix was an old friend of theirs who happened to be a billionaire and owned houses around the world.) We agreed, having no objection to a holiday in such an exotic place as Connecticut. We arranged that when the *Forbes* business was concluded, we would all go together to Connecticut and that they would arrange the transport. Somewhat to my surprise, the transport turned out to be a stretch limo. It appeared that when Felix, a generous chap, loaned you one of his houses, it came complete with the service of limo and driver. The house was beautiful and was supplied with food, drink and a housemaid. The limo driver came round each morning to ask where we would like to go that day. One day, we asked him to drive us round the state, of which we knew nothing. After an hour or two driving mainly through forest, we espied a big open space where there seemed to be a lot of activity. We asked what it was and the driver told us it was a car boot sale. The girls of course said, 'Great. Let's go,' and asked the driver to stop. This he did, though with an air of reluctance. We all got out and, having wandered about and bought sundry items of junk, looked for the limo. The driver was present but not the car. He said in some embarrassment, 'I guess you guys want the limo.'

We of course said 'Yes,' and he brought it from somewhere.

Some time later, when we had come to know him better, he explained: 'In this country, rich folks don't go to car boot sales.'

So, out of mere embarrassment, he had parked the limo out of sight. It is, as I think I may have remarked, another country.

CHAPTER 21

Burns Night

There is a curious Scots tradition which has been going for about two hundred years and which shows no sign of fading. Unlike much Scottish so-called tradition – the kilts and the clan tartans and so on – it has resisted commercialisation and figures neither in the High Street tawdry nor in the itineraries of mass tourism. It is, of course, the Burns Supper: an annual celebration of the life of Scotland's national poet. This resistance is down to the nature of the poet himself, the values he espoused and the inability of the tourism industry to think of a way of making a buck out of poetry. Once a year, throughout Scotland, people gather to dine and drink, to recite poetry and to sing songs, all in honour of a self-taught ploughman. It is, as I say, curious, for I know of no exact parallel in the civilised world.

At its worst, the Burns Supper can be a horror: the prospect of the self-satisfied bourgeois congratulating himself by association with a person, with whom in life he would not choose to associate, is not a pretty sight. It is the expression of a national myth which mythologises a nation for the sake of comfort. But there is more to it than that: it is a requirement of a Burns Supper that poetry be recited and listened to; that speakers speak about the poet and his society, and how the latter treated the former and why. And that the diction of the commentaries be a recognisable variant of the language of the poems, and that it be unforced, for in a nation as close and as critical as Scotland, falsity of tone is instantly discernible.

The format of the occasion is prescribed by custom: it is a relic of the club dinners of the eighteenth century and it may not be varied, save for very good reason. There are speeches and toasts, and every toast must be introduced by a speaker, who is expected to be knowledgeable – and amusing, for at the core of the occasion is conviviality. The food to be eaten is prescribed: it, too, is a relic of another time, for dishes feature that are now little to be seen in supermarket or restaurant. Curiously, there is no parallel prescription of drink, though it would be a strange Burns Supper in which whisky did not make an appearance. Indeed it would be an offence, for the supper is held in honour of the man who wrote Scotch Drink: not the lines from which he derives his immortality, but still expressive of both man and nation.

With the Society well-established and the Members' Room respectable, I had been thinking for some time that we ought to have a Burns Supper. We had contrived to create for the Society an ethos which, though thoroughly Scottish, was unorthodox, left-of-centre and intelligent if not intellectual. We encouraged song and, on occasion, poetry, and if some of our members were self-satisfied and bourgeois, they must have come to us for light relief, for the atmosphere in the Society was neither. Also we saw ourselves (possibly more accurately: I saw us) as being part of a revolution in Scottish popular culture whose pinnacle was the very spirit which we existed to celebrate.

I proposed to our Board that I organise and run a Burns Supper on the 25th of January. Some members were predictably lukewarm and one asked, sceptically, 'Who is to be invited?' I looked at him thoughtfully, and in my mind said, 'Not you, brother.' I explained to the Board that great care would have to be exercised in the issuing of invitations, to avoid a superfluity of folk who would contribute little to the occasion. Thinking as usual on my feet, I said, 'I'll issue the invitations. I guarantee it will be good.' This passed thanks to indifference on the part of the opposition and it came to be acknowledged that it would be the Chairman's Burns Supper. I then proposed that we use the occasion to elect an honorary life member of the Society who would be presented with a case of Society whisky and get a bottle a year for life for 'Services to Scotland'.

'Did you have anyone in mind?' they asked.

I said, 'Yes, Hamish Henderson and David Daiches to start with.'

Some blank looks, though Hamish was the author of the Freedom Come-All-Ye, and David of some forty-odd books including *Scotch Whisky*, which had done more than any other to resuscitate malt whiskies in the sixties. So it was agreed.

It was a toss-up whether the first one should be Hamish or David. I decided Hamish, for he seemed a lot older than David and I wanted to get them both before one of them expired. In fact I was wrong about their respective ages, a matter I explained to David some time later. The bottle a year for life allowed us to make an expansive gesture but wasn't likely to be as expensive as it sounded, both prospective recipients being pretty ancient. So, Hamish it was. When I explained it to him one evening in Sandy Bell's bar, he was, typically, a bit mystified, but mighty pleased – to be on the Tasting Committee *and* to be showered with more whisky seemed beyond reasonable expectation. He thought life membership of the Society a great honour and I was delighted that he accepted, for it was about then that Mrs Thatcher's government had awarded Hamish an MBE or some such accolade – which he sent back with a polite letter declining. There must have been some idiots on the honours committee, even to have thought that Hamish would accept such a thing from Mrs T.

That evening I had gone out looking for him, having phoned his house and got no reply. He wasn't hard to find for, if he were in Edinburgh, Hamish could almost always be found in Sandy Bell's. It was mid-evening when I went in and the pub was fairly empty. I should explain that Sandy Bell's is in two parts, an inner and an outer bar. On entering the door, I could hear a strange yowling noise, which turned out to be made by Hamish and a friend. The friend was a piper and the two of them (both in a state of some inebriation) were exchanging pipe tunes, which they were singing to each other. When the latest pibroch was over I broke in and asked what they were drinking. It was Inchgower, one of UD's lesser-known malts. I bought three more of the same and joined them. Hamish then sang another tune.

'What's that?' asked the piper. 'I never heard that before.'

'I only heard it the once,' replied Hamish. 'It was on the beachhead at Salerno. There was a lot of shell and mortar fire and we were trying to keep our heads down, which wasn't easy, it being a sandy beach. There was a battalion of the Gordons next to us and I heard one of their pipers playing this tune. I thought, there's a brave man, playing a new tune on a beachhead, he might have got it all wrong. But it sounded fine. And then there was a shell burst and I heard it no more.'

What Hamish did not think fit to mention was that, in those same circumstances, he was sufficiently sane to notice an unknown pipe tune and to memorise it well enough to sing it in a pub more than half a century later.

The Burns Supper was a huge success. The Members' Room was packed – or as full as we thought folk could reasonably tolerate. David Daiches gave the Immortal Memory and a wittier, more erudite, more lyrical speech in praise of Rabbie Burns was never heard by me or by anyone else in the room. David had turned down at least a dozen similar invitations to be with us, for he was one of the most sought-after speakers at Burns Suppers – not only in Scotland, but around the world. This was interesting, not because he was one of the world's leading authorities on Burns and Scots literature, but because he was a Jew. His father had come to Edinburgh originally to study the philosophy of David Hume and had liked the country and decided to stay, becoming Scotland's first Rabbi. He was held in great esteem, not only by the small Scottish Jewish community, but by the people of Edinburgh as a whole. That a Jewish community should have found sanctuary in Scotland was to be expected, given the welcome which the Scots have traditionally extended to people of other races and colours. It was also, possibly, due to the fact that a significant part of the Scottish population, being steeped in the Old Testament, thought that they themselves were probably a Lost Tribe of Israel.

I regret to say that I am unable to give a connected account of the four Burns Suppers the Society ran under my aegis; I blame the environment and the whisky, for heroic quantities of the latter were consumed, though without the least disorder. David said to me after the first one that it was the best such event he had ever attended. This from a man of David's distinction was praise indeed – he must have attended a hundred Burns Suppers. Hamish sang several songs, all of his own writing. I recall the Freedom Come-All-Ye and The Banks of Sicily in particular. Margaret Bennett, scholar, singer and folklorist, sang divinely in Scots and in Gaelic, and her son Martyn played brilliantly on four or five different instruments.

One event I do recall, from the first Burns Supper, was the Toast to the Lassies. The speaker (who is always a man) is expected to eulogise the female sex and to propose a toast, to which every man in the room is expected to stand. It is all terribly sexist by present-day standards but if done well it should give no offence and be located firmly in that atmosphere of mutual acceptance which characterises all decent society. But it has to be handled sensitively and intelligently if those criteria are to be met, and I knew there were women among us who would tolerate nothing less.

I had thought these requirements would be met if I asked my friend Michael to give the first of the Society's Toasts to the Lassies. Michael is a very clever guy, a historian of distinction, a bon viveur and a wit. He is also a Tory and a scourge of simplistic leftist critiques of Scottish history, which meant he would probably disagree with quite a lot of the other guests, which would make for balance. Though a bachelor he was happy to do the speech, and my mind was easy on that account.

I was less easy when, after a little while, Michael began to misbehave. He had drunk far more than he ought and was generally making himself objectionable, which made me apprehensive about his toast. He even contrived to be annoying during David's speech, which was frankly intolerable, for a greater gentleman than David never lived. So, shortly before Michael was to speak, I had come to the conclusion that he must not do so. The problem was how? I was pondering this among all the chatter when I caught the eye of an old friend sitting nearby. He was Owen Hand. As a young man, Owen had sailed on one of the last whaling ships to sail from Leith to the Antarctic. He had been a folk singer in the early days – and a lovely singer he was, too. Now, in middle age, he was massively built and dressed in a white tuxedo. Having caught Owen's eye, I glanced to my right, where Michael was behaving like a schoolboy, and then glanced toward the door. Owen understood immediately and, when Michael got up to go to the toilet, Owen followed him. A few minutes later, he returned and nodded to me. This was fine, but I was now without a speaker and would have to do it myself.

I have never made a more successful speech in my life. I

began by announcing that the scheduled speaker had had to be thrown out for drunkenness and bad behaviour, at which there were cheers all round, for I hadn't been the only one to notice. Then I had to think of something to say. I forget exactly what – but I needn't have worried, for if I had read them the *Sunday Post* I would have got an ovation. Then we had the announcement of Hamish's award, and Hamish's reply, which was brilliant. Then songs, then 'Tam o' Shanter', then more songs. Then 'Holy Willie', I forget by whom (the recitation, that is, not the authorship). I won't say there were no sore heads in the morning, but there were fewer than there would have been had it been whisky of lesser quality.

The following year it was David's turn to receive the honorary life membership. I should perhaps tell you a very little about him. (A pity, because there is so much to tell.) The most important thing as regards whisky is his book, titled simply *Scotch Whisky, Its Past and Present*. The book was timely, perceptive and accurate, as well as lyrical, and it followed Neil Gunn in deploring the necessity – which the distillers apparently perceived – of bottling few of the malt whiskies. Doing the research for this book took David to many distilleries – at a time when the public was rarely admitted and a whisky drinker would as soon have thought of visiting a monastery. One day, David visited Bowmore, on Islay, having written to seek permission. He said the management could not have been more welcoming and he was shown all he wished to see. At the end of the tour he was taken to the sample room where Stanley P. Morrison, whose family owned the distillery, offered him a dram. The dram was of a well-known blended whisky, in which Bowmore figured prominently. David asked if he might try the malt by itself and, of course, they poured him a glass. He sipped it and declared it excellent. At that point – and I quote David exactly – Mr Morrison asked if it were nice on its own. David naturally said yes, so his host tried it and said with surprise that indeed it was very pleasant. The conclusion, though unavoidable, is astonishing: the owner of the distillery had never thought of drinking his product as a single malt. In 1968. All the whisky he ever drank was blended. That shows how far we have come.

Another illustration, though nothing this time to do with whisky. I had been to the theatre to see *The Cherry Orchard* for the second or third time and was as bored as I had been before. The next day David and I met at the Society, and I asked him, 'David, tell me about Chekhov. What am I missing? Is he as good as they say he is?'

He smiled. 'Yes, probably,' he said. 'I first read him in German and I was so impressed that I learned Russian with the sole purpose of reading Chekhov in the original.'

'Oh,' I said.

He offered to give me an introduction to Chekhov which he had written but I reckoned it would have been wasted – there was no fear I would consent to *The Cherry Orchard* again.

Subsequent Burns Suppers blur together in memory. But they were alike in their high spirits and joyfulness. We next gave a life membership to the poet Norman MacCaig. Norman had the unusual ability to be very funny while looking miserable. His humour was of rather a cerebral sort and I, at least, would sometimes find myself laughing at something he said hours afterward, when it dawned on me just what he had meant. Norman gave a speech which fitted my description exactly. The rest of the guests must have been sharper than I was, for he was received with cheers without any delay. Or maybe they didn't care and just thought he was such a good old boy that they would have cheered him if he had recited the Gospels – which I'm sure he was capable of doing. The next year we gave the accolade to an economist, not just to be ecumenical, but because he was a very good chap. He was, of course, Ken Alexander, whom I have described elsewhere.

After that, I'm sorry to say, careful management took over and the practice was discontinued.

A short Daiches anecdote, if I may, which shows how small a country Scotland is. I have an old and dear friend called John Maclean. John is descended from one of the Mull Macleans and some years ago, to his delight, discovered that one of his direct ancestors had gone by the charming title of Red Hector of the Battles. Happily, the aggression has been diluted over the last few centuries and a more peaceable chap than John you couldn't meet. All our lives are the outcomes of accidents, but some produce more interesting results than others. John, I'm not sure why, became expert in the restoration of ancient textiles, and for years made a living by it, working in big houses where old but valuable carpets required conservation.

One day, John received a phone call from an old lady who lived in Sciennes. Sciennes is an area on the south side of Edinburgh, which derives its name from a Dominican convent built there in 1517 after the battle of Flodden, at the behest of some of the ladies whose husbands had found the English not to be the walkover they expected. (We Scots make a great to-do about the battle of Bannockburn, at which we were victorious over the English, but little is said about Flodden, at which the flower of Scotland was slaughtered and Edinburgh seriously depopulated.) From the early nineteenth century, Sciennes was where most of Edinburgh's Jewish population lived, including the Daiches family.

This old lady, who was Jewish, had a lot of very fine carpets, most of which were in poor condition, and she wanted John's expert opinion about what she might do with them. John gave her his opinion and ended up repairing a great many of them and losing money because of it – but that's the sort of guy he is. When he had finished the job, which took months, the old lady insisted on giving him a carpet which she said had been brought to Edinburgh in the nineteenth century by Rabbi Daiches. (My spellcheck just wrote Rabbie Daiches. Let's be clear, Scotland's national poet was not a Jewish clergyman.)

The carpet is a lovely thing. It is a Persian garden carpet in silk and wool, probably made in Isfahan more than a hundred years ago. Its principal colours are red and green, though the green has faded. It is very fragile indeed and John had it on the wall of his big flat in Thirlestane Road. When he moved house, as he did about twenty years ago, to Iona, a small island on Scotland's west coast, he realised his little cottage would have no place for the Daiches carpet, and so he gave it to me. I had it on the wall of my house for about twenty years, until we, too, moved to a house which lacked the perfect place for the carpet. It lay rolled up under a bed for a couple of years until my conscience got the better of me. Whatever was to be the fate of such a lovely carpet, it shouldn't be lying under a bed. Nor could I in decency sell it; so far it had changed hands for love and I wasn't going to be the one who broke the chain. Furthermore David Daiches, I'm proud to say, had been a friend of mine.

Jenni Daiches, David's daughter, had been married to Angus Calder, son of Ritchie, and, finding a number for her, I called. She was a little surprised; as she said, it's not every day an old friend calls out of the blue and offers to restore, gratis, to your family a valuable heirloom, but yes, she would be happy to have it. So one day I put it in the car and drove south. I must say, I'm happy to be shot of it – some things are just too much of a responsibility.

CHAPTER 22

Bernard

John Mackintosh was a friend of mine. He was the best and ablest politician Scotland has produced in many generations. John held Berwick and East Lothian for Labour, despite its being a naturally Tory constituency, because all the people in the landward, areas who would normally have voted Tory, voted for him simply because anyone could see he was a gentleman and he talked common sense. For years, on Sunday mornings, John would write a piece which the *Scotsman* newspaper would print on its centre page on the Monday. He would take a situation of current interest which most of us had only the haziest idea about; he would explain why it had come about, and what ought to be done about it. You came away thinking you ought to have known how simple the business was and congratulating yourself on now understanding it – whereas you should really have been congratulating John. On more than one occasion, in John's house at Nether Liberton, I have come downstairs on a Sunday morning with a hangover after the previous night's discussion, to find John in his library, writing his *Scotsman* piece with a fountain pen. When it was done, he would blot the ink, fold the paper, put it in an envelope and give it to his young son, Stuart, who would cycle down to the North Bridge and put it through the *Scotsman*'s letterbox.

In addition to being an assiduous MP and looking after the welfare of his constituents, John also managed to bring up a young family, stay married to Una, write the definitive book on the British Constitution, edit *Political Quarterly*, write lots of articles and academic papers, and be Professor of Politics at Edinburgh University. And what is more, he thought that it was the business of the professor to inspire his students, so he took it upon himself to deliver all the lectures of the First Ordinary Politics course at nine o'clock in the morning. Most nine o'clock lectures were sparsely attended: at John's it was standing room only. In addition, he was lots of fun and in his leisure, though he was acceptable to the greatest in the land, he liked to get together with his old friends, of whom I had the privilege of being one. It was a tragedy when he died at forty-eight: for his family, his friends and for the nation.

John left a huge library and one of his colleagues, Bernard Crick, who had the politics chair at Birkbeck College in London University, came north to catalogue it. Bernard, who retired about then, got on well with the cataloguing, and with Una, John's widow. So well, indeed, that he decided to move to Edinburgh. Bernard had a pretty good opinion of himself and could be amusing when he pleased, both of which, together with his scholarly reputation, endeared him to a certain section of Edinburgh society. I liked Bernard, whom I found absurd. I'm not sure whether he liked me: I think he did, though he would take umbrage when I laughed at him, which I did pretty often.

Bernard became a member of the syndicate and, eventually, of the Board of the Society. He was pleased about both, though he was useless as a company director. He seemed unable to grasp the notion that the purpose of the Board of a company is to conduct its business. Bernard treated it as a debating society and would be displeased when I or anyone else tried to cut one of his monologues short by pointing out that the issue on which he was discoursing was of no importance and that there were other, more pressing things, requiring attention. He persevered for years, though, and we were all sorry when he died.

In Bernard's later years, I owned a Norwegian pilot boat which I had found lying in southern Portugal and which I was having expensively repaired at a yard near the Spanish border. (Over the years I owned a number of boats, and had a taste for very old boats, most of which required extensive repair when they came into my hands. Sailing is notorious for being expensive, but compared to the restoration of old wooden boats, let me tell you that yachts are cheap.) For this particular boat I needed two wooden masts and I was not confident of the ability of the yard to source timber of the requisite quality, so I decided to have the masts made in Scotland and (somehow) transported to the Algarve.

I had already fabricated several masts, so I knew what I was about. The first problem was to find the right trees. There are lots of trees which will do for a boat's mast, but not a lot you would want to rely on in a hard blow, so the selection of the timber is crucial. And there isn't that much first-class timber about. I had asked Mackay's yard in Arbroath to do the job and they said, 'You had better talk to Charlie Riddel,' and gave me directions. Charlie is a man of about retirement age and, though he talks a lot about it, it is plain that he has little intention of ever retiring. He has a small sawmill near Forfar where he divides his time between splitting logs and chatting to his many friends and acquaintances. It is always a pleasure to visit him because the chat is good and the new-sawn timber smells delicious. Charlie appears to be acquainted with most trees of any substance in the northern part of Scotland. I took my problem to Charlie and he said he would see what he could do, promising to ring me, and I left.

A few weeks later I took a call. The caller did not announce himself but the voice left me in no doubt: 'I've found twa sticks that might do ye,' he said. 'Ower by Pitlochry. Dae ye want tae see them?'

I replied in the affirmative. 'When?' I asked.

'On Sunday,' he said.

I agreed and it was duly arranged that I would drive over and pick Charlie up, and that the two of us would go to Pitlochry. It was a fine morning and on the way Charlie would occasionally point to a mountain and say things like: 'I took ten thousand ton of Sitka spruce off of that hill.' Sometimes we talked about other masts Charlie had procured and the surprisingly low level of intelligence to be found among young men pretending to a knowledge of timber. But the weather was mild and the day lovely and the road from Forfar to Pitlochry has few equals anywhere, so the time passed agreeably. Besides, I was genuinely interested in the effect of a spiral grain in the timber of a mast. That's not something you find in a general knowledge quiz on the television.

From Pitlochry (or was it Dunkeld? I forget, no matter) we took a side road. That part of Highland Scotland is heavily forested and, unlike most Scots forest, it is quite old, with lots of mature trees. The landscape looks entirely natural but anyone who knows forestry (I'm told) can tell that it is managed, and well-managed, too. The forest is mostly but not entirely coniferous, and these come in many different species. The side road led us through the trees for some miles until we stopped in a clearing where we had arranged to meet the forester and owner. The latter and the former were combined in one man, sandy-haired, lean and tall, in early middle-age. Charlie introduced us: his name was Barbour, a name which goes back into the mists of early Scottish history.

My requirements had already been explained. He said, 'There is a stand of Norway spruce not far from here which has some good trees that might do you.'

We got into his Land Rover and drove through the forest for about twenty minutes. We stopped before a conical hill covered with very tall trees. With the sun shining on it, the hill would have made a good illustration for a fairy tale. Now, if you have any experience of selecting trees for straightness, you will know that, though the overall impression of forest conifers is one of perfect perpendicularity, when you look at them closely you see that every tree is bent in one way or another. Really straight ones are the exception – and for the mast of a boat, it does need to be straight. This whole hill was an exception to my rule. Almost every tree on it would have made a perfect mast. Mr Barbour said, 'I have marked the two I thought best, but if you prefer any others, just say.' I looked more closely. Among the brown of the trunks and the green of the leaves (needles, really) were, incongruously, two yellow ribbons, each tied round a tree-trunk. After a brief inspection, I said, 'Those will do fine, thank you.'

I don't know who organised Bernard's funeral, but it wasn't me. I expect it must have been his family: nobody else would have had the cheek. A few years before he died, Bernard had moved to Bellevue Terrace, part of the later New Town, a few minutes' walk from our house. It had been arranged that the mourners would meet at Bernard's house and proceed thence to the crematorium, which is about half a mile away. We walked over that morning and joined a large number of friends, who had all known Bernard. We were told by whoever was organising things, that we would all walk to the crematorium behind the hearse. This was unusual but, so far, not surprising. What was surprising, was the marching band which, following the hearse, led the funeral procession. Not a pipe band, as you might have expected in Edinburgh, but a New Orleans jazz band. The sheer absurdity of the thing was inescapable but, all were agreed, perfectly appropriate.

I found myself walking beside Charlotte, whom I had known since she was a child. Charlotte was the daughter of my deceased friend, John Mackintosh. With her was her husband, Freeland, who is a fine musician, whom I had met a few times, but not often. The morning was quiet and sunny and we chatted as we walked along, rather enjoying the unhappiness of the traffic which had to halt to let us past. Charlotte asked what I had been up to since last we had met, some years before. Being not long back from the mast-seeking expedition to Pitlochry, I told them about it. I enthused about the lovely place and its admirable owner. Freeland smiled and his reply astonished me.

'I know it well,' he said. 'I gave it to him. He's my brother. I had no use for a Highland estate.'

Chapter 23

Boats

If you have read this far, you will know that when I wasn't doing anything else, I was likely to be found on, or under, a boat – more often under than on. You will also know that my preference in boats runs to elderly, wooden ones. I'm not a snob about this, unlike many old-boat buffs: I like modern boats fine. Indeed, when I'm on a plastic boat, especially in the wet, I have been known to swear that never again will I inhabit a craft which lets water in through the seams of hull and deck. But it never lasts. I think it's to do with love, that leap of the heart with which you perceive the object of desire. For me, apart from women, it's dirty old boats that do it. (The women in my life may think this uncomplimentary: it is not so intended. In my emotional life the two are quite unconnected. The actresses to whom I have adverted above, who tarred the bottom of the *Clan Gordon*, were merely a happy accident and nothing to do with my emotions.) The connections between boats and whisky were also for the most part accidental – though for a while surprisingly constant, like the actresses.

The *Gannet*, which I have mentioned earlier, was not my first boat. That was an eighteen-foot lugger which, at the age of fifteen, I bought for five pounds. She was built in the traditional Scottish style, of larch planks on oak frames and she carried a single mast. She had no name and no engine, being referred to by me simply as 'the boat', and by everyone else as 'Pip's boat'. The lack of an engine was a severe handicap, given that I kept her on the River Carron, a tributary of the Forth. On one bank of the river lay the docks and on the other, an expanse of mudbanks stretching all the way to the Kincardine Bridge five miles away. The tides flowed fast over the flats and the lack of an engine was a serious disadvantage, but a second-hand Seagull outboard then cost five pounds and, since I had given all I had for the boat and there was no prospect of any more, I had to learn to sail her with no means of propulsion other than the sails. Since none of my friends were remotely interested in sailing (they wanted fags and Rock 'n' Roll) I also had to learn to sail her single-handed. I did not own a life-jacket: indeed it did not occur to me that I might.

I learned quickly, as one does when drowning is in prospect. One day, going down the river on the ebb, the boat stuck on the mud. I dropped the sail to stop her going further and tried to push her off using an oar. When that didn't work, and with the ebbing tide it was obvious I would get marooned, I stripped off and jumped into the muddy water. As soon as I did so, relieved of my weight the boat bobbed up. I was just about to shove her off when I realised that if I lost hold of her, I would be left with mud to my knees and water to my waist and unable to move, for the mud was glutinous. So, clinging to the transom, I managed slowly to extract one foot after another from the mud and push her into slightly deeper water and climb back on board. It was a small incident but it did make me aware (I think for the first time) that I might get myself drowned.

It wasn't all mudlarking, though, and when she did sail, the boat went beautifully. The lug sail was cumbersome, but it set well. (I would appreciate this only many years later.) It was at that time, I think, that I had an intense vision of the sheer beauty of a boat – any boat – moving through still water. It's not something I can explain, but it is still with me. I can go down to the harbour and see one of the great oil-rig supply boats leave its mooring, or watch a child's toy boat on a pond, and I experience again the emotion I had more than half a century before.

If I need an explanation of my liking for boats in general, that is it. That I should feel strongly about old boats, probably comes from the same place. When autumn came, I had the boat pulled up onto the slip of the little yacht club. The planks dried out over the winter and, come the spring, I found that the planks had sprung away from the stem, rendering the boat unusable. I knew nothing about such things so naturally sought the advice of grown men who could be presumed to know. In the yacht club everyone I asked seemed to be highly knowledgeable, and they all said the same thing.

'It's knackered, son. Ye might as well burn it.'

'But isn't there some way to fix it?' I would ask.

'No,' they all replied.

Their unanimity and certainty were impenetrable. I grieved. There wasn't much else I could do, for I was unable to imagine how a repair might be effected.

If I were faced with such a problem today, it might take me a day's work to make a few templates from which to fashion an apron behind the stem, to bolt the apron through the stem and then, one at a time, to cramp the planks up to the stem and fasten each with a nail to the apron. Paint, caulk and pay, and paint again – job done. But at that time all I could do was grieve and the boat died of my ignorance. It seems a trivial thing to determine how I would spend a part of my life, but I think that we have little choice in such matters – and I don't complain, for I had a lot of fun out of it even if I did get wet in the process of losing a lot of money. And it taught me to be sceptical of the certainties of people who think they know.

Dick Morton must take some of the blame for my obsession with boats or would, if he were still with us. As I mentioned earlier, when he got the job in Papua New Guinea, he rang me one day and asked, 'Would you like to have the *Gannet*?' I didn't need a boat – nobody ever *needs* a boat in that sense – but I couldn't refuse. Also, I was doing Dick a favour, for he had been converting the *Gannet* from a ship's lifeboat to a cabin cruiser with the intention of sailing her around the world. Knowing Dick, if nothing had intervened he would have done just that. Or he would have tried to, for his carpentry was about the standard you might expect of a Cambridge don and his knowledge of boats was much the same – i.e. long on book learning and short on practicalities. But he was bold and generous.

I have already told you of one venture in the *Gannet*. After that, my mobility was compromised for some time and boats out of the question, so she went to a new owner who treated her well. Some years later I found the *Clan Gordon* lying ashore in Tayport. I had had an interest in sailing fishing boats and I had been looking around to see if there were any Zulus left in Scotland. The Zulu, I should tell you briefly, is a type of fishing boat developed on the east coast of Scotland in the third quarter of the nineteenth century. They were lovely boats, pointed at both ends and heavily built of larch planks on oak frames. They carried two masts which had no stays, for they set lug sails, which won't set properly on a stayed mast. The masts in consequence were immense, as were the sails. (When steam engines were first brought into the Scottish fishing fleet, they weren't used for propulsion, but for raising the sails, and for hauling the nets.) The boats sailed wonderfully well. They were, though, very big. They were introduced around the time of the battle of Isandlwana, hence the name (the Scottish public on the whole thought the Zulus must be pretty fine chaps, to have defeated a British army, even a small one).

I was excited, for the *Clan Gordon* appeared to be a Zulu, though just under forty feet long. She was, in fact, a Loch Fyne skiff, a class of boat developed for the herring fishing on Loch Fyne, whose hull was modelled on the Zulu. I bought her, though she was a wreck, and had her brought down to Granton where I rebuilt her. As I said earlier, I estimated the job would take me eighteen months, but it took ten years. It involved the purchase, not of timber but of trees. The engine I built out of two piles of scrap. One had lain for years on the pier at Stornoway; the other was the remains of the engines of the Forth pilot launches from the 1930s. Out of them I built a working J4 Kelvin diesel, as sweet an engine as anyone ever saw. But it was the mast I thought I might tell you about in more detail. Anyone who has plenty of money can get a mast: you go to a boatbuilder and you wave a wad of readies in front of him and say 'Mast'. There's no fun in that – though I must admit it has advantages in terms of economy of time.

When I was up to about year eight of the rebuild, I bent my mind to the business of procuring a mast by means other than pecuniary. I began, as I began most things, by asking my friends. As I may have said, I was blessed with a wide acquaintance, and I cast around among them for someone who might have access to a suitable tree, preferably close to water, for ease of transport. I held out the possibility of bottles of overproof whisky as well as, or instead of, payment in currency.

One evening, over a discussion of the merits of Ardbeg *vis-à-vis* Lagavulin, my friend Jamie came up with a suggestion. Now if you are Scottish and you know that Jamie is male, you also know that his parents were either upper class or antiquarian, or both, for Jamie is the diminutive of James and is now used in Scotland only by posh people or conscious antiquarians. All the other Jameses are called Jimmy. (There is

216

a tiny third form of Jamesie which we owe mainly to my old friend Tony Roper, who invented him as a sidekick for Rab C. Nesbitt, but I digress.)

Jamie said, 'I think I know who might have a tree that would suit you – and in a convenient place.'

'Who is that, and where?' I enquired.

'The Earl of Mar', Jamie said. 'He's a friend of mine, and I shall be seeing him in the House of Lords next week. He has a small forest near Alloa, full of pines and larches.' (I told you Jamie would be posh. He is a hereditary peer, hence the House of Lords.)

So it was arranged that Jamie would ask his friend; the friend was most obliging and word was passed to his forester to expect a call from me. I rang and a visit to the forest was arranged. I picked out a fine larch. The forester obligingly offered to fell it and I said I would arrange the transport.

Again, if money is no object, transporting a forty-foot stick is not a problem, but nor, it has to be said, is it likely to produce much in the way of fun. You just wave the cash in front of the owner of a low-loader, who will in time deliver it. But that would be feeble as well as expensive, and lacking in the warmth of human fellowship. So I discussed my problem with my friend Davy Brand. Davy fishes creels for lobsters and crabs, working out of Newhaven harbour, and in winter he fishes whelks, or snottery buckies, which he sells to an Irishman who, I believe, sends them to South Korea. Given the proximity of the noble earl's forest to the river, Davy was able to arrange the matter.

On an agreed day, I took a Land Rover to Alloa, a small industrial town on the upper Forth. From Alloa I made my way to the forest, which was not far outside the town. The tree was awaiting me, shorn of its branches and forty-five feet long. The river was a mile or so away, so all we had to do was get it there. There was a small slipway, now disused, which had the distinction of having its own public house – being within the purview of the Earl of Mar's lands, it was wonderfully known as the Mars Bar. Our problem was how to get the forty-five-foot stick to the Mars Bar. Short of a long trailer – which could have been procured but would have taken time and money – the only thing to do was to attach one end of the stick to the tow-hitch and simply drag it to the water. Its length was six feet more than I needed and I reckoned that the abrasion caused by the end rubbing on the tarmac couldn't remove that much. So off we set.

Our route took us by a country road to a council housing estate on the edge of Alloa, but it only skirted the housing and thereafter it was a short distance to the river. All went well and the Land Rover drove remarkably well, considering it was towing a tree, until I heard behind me the now familiar sound of a police car in earnest. You may have guessed that at this point I had a feeling of *déjà vu*. The parallel could not have been closer. The policeman was evidently at a loss for the exact statute which we might be shown to have violated, but was serious. Just to show willing, I got out of the Land Rover. Explanations followed. Our destination, which was all of a hundred yards away, was indicated. The attachment to the tow-hitch was examined – it was secure. I gave an assurance that the tree had been paid for. Polis grumpy, deprived of an arrest on a quiet Sunday morning, but unable to think of an offence said, 'OK. Carry on.'

It being Sunday, the Mars Bar was closed, even for the sale of chocolate bars, which was a disappointment. I had, however, brought a bottle or three, for use as currency or consolation, or both. Davy's friend arrived. The friend ran a workboat which acted as safety cover for the construction of the new Kincardine bridge. He towed our stick to the bridge and Davy, obliging man, took his lobster boat up the river and fetched it down to Granton. There were celebrations as we hauled it up on the Corinthian slip and the Society provided the means of celebration.

There were several other boats about this time. I have mentioned the *Kami no Michi*, though not the occasion on which she narrowly avoided becoming a wreck. I won't go into that one, save to say it is the only occasion on which I have ever called for assistance. I was in the *Kami* with one helpless crew member, at night on a lee shore in a hard gale with a disabled engine and no battery power for my radio. I also had a badly sprained ankle and could use only one leg, so I didn't feel too bad about being a nuisance. Assistance was provided by the Buckie lifeboat, to whose crew I later sent a dozen bottles of Society whisky. I got a very friendly note from the secretary saying really I shouldn't have bothered, but the chaps all said thanks very much and if I ever wanted to be shipwrecked again, please be sure to do it off Cullen Head.

CHAPTER 24

Leaving

Now we come to the painful bit: how I left the Society and why. Neil Wilson, the decent man, wrote a piece a few weeks ago about me and the Society in which, in a kindly euphemism, he referred to my retiring from its chairmanship. It wasn't like that, I'm sorry to say. I didn't jump: I was pushed. Whether this was a good thing or not is a matter of opinion. I'm not even sure, myself, which side of the opinion I come down on.

One thing is sure, the Society at that time generated a quite extraordinary amount of emotion among the people who were involved with it. And naturally, since emotion is no promoter of objectivity, a lot of things got forgotten which ought not to have been. And, just as naturally, being the founder and chairman of the company, I found myself the focus of most of the emotion – which perhaps reduced even my renowned ability to remain objective. But time dulls the edge of the razor of regret and in what follows I will tell you how things appeared to me as best I can.

From fairly early in the history of the Society, there was a divergence of attitude among the members of the Board of

Directors. There were those who saw it as a little, local outfit, which might make a few wavelets in a very small pond but would not otherwise cause much of a stir. And there were a few of us who saw the possibility that the thing might be made to fly. As I have said, I had discovered a seam of pure gold which only I had thought of mining. The possibilities were immense. I ask you, if you had struck such metal, what would you do? Would you creep around until all the surrounding miners – the big corporations – came to understand the value of what you had found and then took it from you? I could see that might happen sooner or later – for the supply to the Society of first-class casks depended on the owners of those casks remaining unaware of the market we had created – and I knew we must grasp the opportunity quickly. I took it upon myself to realise that immense possibility and from the beginning was content to leave the implementation to others.

It may be worth mentioning at this point that from the beginning, though I had started the thing and I was driving it, I was content to take a back seat as far as the Board of Directors was concerned. It was with some surprise that I found that there were people who thought that being chairman of the Scotch Malt Whisky Society was a big deal, so I was content to cede the position to one after another, all of whom proved to be earthbound. Eventually I saw that if flight were to be possible, I would have to take the position myself. That wasn't easy, for I had begun the company as I had the syndicate, on a basis of equal shareholdings. (To any normal company promoter no doubt this sounds naïve, but you should remember that I had conceived the whole thing as a co-operative venture.) When I was young I had read Machiavelli and Castiglione and I had been involved in politics, so at Board meetings I usually carried my point, but not, it has to be said, without making some enemies.

The division among the directors was roughly between those who, like me, saw how much could be done, and those who wished things to stay exactly as they were. Alas, we ended up with rather a lot of the latter – I think perhaps because most of the livelier people already had busy lives to lead and didn't have time or inclination to run a business. But there was also a social side to our disagreements. Having begun the business by stealing from under their noses the finest product of the Scotch whisky industry, I was inclined to be somewhat disrespectful of the establishment; what those guys wanted to do, was to *join* it. You must remember that in Scotland and in places like golf clubs, being a director of a whisky company – even an unorthodox one – carried a social cachet. It was not a creative tension and it produced a situation in which, when good advice *was* offered, I was disinclined to take it.

Hence my reputation for headstrong, if charismatic, leadership. The differences were such that it became increasingly difficult for me to get agreement to almost any development. Let me give an example. For years after the building became habitable, the grand chamber which is now our Members' Room lay vacant. When I proposed that it be turned into a members' bar, and used for tastings, I met strong resistance. The naysayers said nay, as naysayers do. 'It will cost a fortune to fit it out and it will never make money,' they said. It is now, if I am not mistaken, the spiritual core, the heart of a worldwide Society – but it was a struggle.

Despite the resistance, though, leading the Society was enjoyable. Those of us who were driving it forward were having a lot of fun, whereas the conservative, stick-in-the-mud faction were not. Why this was so is not for me to say, but I think it has a lot to do with character and attitude – some folk have fun and some do not. I was quite sure that, if the Society were to be successful, it would be because people thought that it was fun. OK, so it was irresponsible, but not very, and people were attracted by that very air of irresponsibility.

It was certainly a very different thing from a lot of

self-important old men quaffing spirits (neat because, being old, they are unable to smell them) and congratulating themselves on being connoisseurs. I'm happy to say that, under the present management, the Society has leaned strongly in the former direction – and it has taken the aged with it, to their great benefit.

For a good many years, membership of the Society in the UK grew steadily. People were attracted by the story and the sheer quality of the whisky, and the latter acted as a guarantee of the veracity of the former. It was a virtuous circle. Added to which we were having a good time, and it showed, and people responded to that, too – for remember, it was the 1980s and there wasn't a lot of fun about. Often foreigners would turn up at The Vaults and ask, 'Why can't I get this stuff in the USA, in France, in Germany, in Japan? When are you going to go international?' After Anne left, in Denise Neilson we found a lively, go-ahead managing director who was keen to make things happen both at home and abroad. And Denise was fun, too.

I have written above about the US venture, which went well, though the cash didn't come in quickly enough to cover our costs and for years we were out of pocket. We also sent Tim Steward, one of our directors who spoke Japanese, to Tokyo, to open a branch there. Alas, at the time Japan, which hitherto had been booming, was on the brink of the recession from which its economy has yet to recover, so we lost money on that too. Looking back, it's easy to see that I should have installed stronger financial management about then, but our bank was supportive, indeed enthusiastic, and happy to give us whatever overdraft facilities we required. Money being easy to get, we could see no reason not to go for growth.

It soon became apparent that the company needed more cash if it were to realise its ambitions. We organised a share offer to our members, which brought in a bit, but not enough. So I got together with an old friend, Adrian Darke, and together we bought up the balance of the share offer, effectively bank-rolling our bets on the company's future. When Denise left, Adrian became MD for a while. Adrian was from a different world: he sold computers. I don't mean he had a little shop selling PCs: he fitted out major airports with complete systems for megabucks. I recall one day, as were passing through Singapore airport, Adrian looked down about half a mile of check-in desks and remarked, 'I sold them that lot.' I think he never quite adjusted to the small scale of our operation, and, after a bit, he went back to doing what made him money. I then hired a chap called Richard Gordon, who had worked for Glenmorangie, and was keen to do the job. Under Richard, the whole operation began to look less rackety, though he found the discord on the Board stressful.

Still, things seemed to be going well. We stopped the haem-orrhage of cash, and prospects were good both at home and overseas, though the overdraft stayed stubbornly high. I was pretty confident we were over the hill. And then our bank manager, who had been supportive all along, went away (I forget why). He was replaced by some creep from head office (by then in London), who took a look at our account and decided he didn't like what he saw. We had various meetings to try to convince him, but to no avail. We looked around for alternative sources of finance, but found none. The rest is a bit of a blur. Board meetings were called, shareholders formed cabals and talked to the bank; eventually a compromise was reached whereby the bank would support a rescue, but at the expense, of course, of my head. It all happened quite quickly.

Richard had a family to support and a career to think about, so naturally he went where he saw a future. There was a meeting at which I was offered a titular position of President of the Society, or some such demeaning dignity with no influence, to be wheeled out to pontificate to geriatric members. Naturally, I told them to get lost. That's about it. You may imagine with what feelings I watched as, a few years later, those paragons of fiscal rectitude and commercial acumen, our bankers, the Royal Bank of Scotland, went to the wall – or would have done, had not a Labour government, which they detested, nationalised them.

Chapter 25

Afterwords

Though leaving the company I had spent so many years creating was a shock, it was not a surprise, and I had given some thought to what I might do with the rest of my life. Evidently, I would need to make a living; equally evidently there was probably nobody in the whisky industry who would employ me, had I had any desire for employment, which I did not: you can tame young animals, but not old ones. What I had in mind was a book, perhaps more than one.

It may have been apparent from the foregoing that I find organised falsehood annoying. I don't think this is the outcome of natural virtue so much as irritation that, in things I care about, so many people should have been misled for so long by so few. In the years since I had started the Society, I had naturally sought to understand how it was possible that we should have been able to do what we did, and I had embodied my findings in a work entitled *Scots on Scotch*. This was a volume of essays about Scotland and whisky, written mostly by my friends, with an introduction by me. In the latter I describe how a fake version of Scottish culture was used by the Scotch whisky industry to convince the drinking public that the only whisky worth drinking was blended whisky of a generally inferior sort. If this interests you, it was published by Mainstream and your best course is to get a copy and read it.

The book I really had in mind was to become *Appreciating Whisky*. This arose from my response to another but different irritation: the tendency of most books about whisky to say little about the only things that make it worth drinking in the first place – its flavour and its propensity to inebriate. There isn't a lot of mystery about the latter; the more you drink, the drunker you get. But the origins of whisky flavour were a largely untouched field, so I wrote about that. I had a lot of help with the book, from people who knew a great deal more about it than I did. It was also a lot of fun doing the research, as you may imagine. HarperCollins undertook to publish it, mainly, I think, at the urging of one of their star authors, and did a fine job of the production. There is little point in rehearsing the book's arguments here: enough to say that it was well received by the then-growing band of malt enthusiasts as well as by the industry. The latter had begun to awake from their long sleep and brands were appearing which were plainly influenced by what we had done at the Whisky Society. I see the book has recently been reprinted and is now generally available. If its publishers feel inclined to pay the copyright royalties which are due, I can be reached c/o the Whisky Society.

My next venture was to do the same for wine. I collected all the books I could find about wine and read some of them. (Lots of them were unreadable for the same reason that lots of books about whisky are unreadable.) To my astonishment I found that very rarely was there mention of flavour and, even more rarely, of how the wines got their flavour. So there had to be a market for my approach, even though in the matter of wine I was a relative beginner.

I spent an enjoyable year or two doing the research. There

had been plenty of research done on the origins of wine flavour, though few of the results had been made available to the public. No doubt the vintners thought, as did the distillers, that the public didn't want to know. The people who make the stuff certainly are laudably concerned and wherever I went, were more than pleased to tell me of their findings. I toured vineyards and wineries across Europe and America, and wherever I went I found, especially among the young, a concern for quality.

Just occasionally my wine researches would coincide with my whisky interests. As when Macallan asked me if I would like to look at what they had done in Spain and offered to meet expenses. They flew me to Jerez, where they are part-owners of a cooperage which makes casks for sherry. The sherry matures the casks and the casks in turn mature the whisky. It is as neat a business arrangement as you could hope to meet, and it's the real thing, quite devoid of bullshit – as you would expect of Macallan. The trip to Jerez came most opportunely, for I had intended to tour the Rioja province in company with my daughter, Stephanie, who would act as my translator, for my Spanish is pitiful. I therefore flew from Jerez to Barcelona, hired a car and off we went.

Let me tell you that if you want to get the attention of Spanish wine makers, there can be no better combination than an old man travelling with his beautiful daughter. Spanish men are as responsive as any to a good-looking woman, but wary of intruding on a relationship. But a father travelling with his daughter is a guarantee of respectability on the part of both, and both may be approached with the courtesy which is an established custom of the country. Our trip was doubly a success – we had a great time and we tasted a lot of good wines. I can't say I learned a lot I couldn't have got from books, but we did lay the ground for a chapter on Rioja.

The work I did for *Appreciating Whisky* made me realise that there was scope for a more adventurous work on the subject.

This too was to be about the flavour of whiskies, but from a different angle. The idea was to analyse the flavours present in a whisky; to do so in as scientifically objective a way as possible, and to present the results by means of a graphic which would enable the consumer to tell at a glance whether a given whisky would be to his or her taste. It was to be titled *The Scotch Whisky Directory* and it was intended to cover malt and blended whiskies impartially, for by then I had realised that some people were cashing in on the fashion for malts and bottling single malt whiskies which were inferior to quite ordinary blends, but much more expensive. It was a fairly ambitious project, but I had been thinking about it for some time and talking to people who knew about the things I would need. Mainstream offered to publish it.

The first requirement was someone to taste the whiskies. I asked around the people I knew in the industry: who are the four best noses? The responses were fairly uniform: in no particular order, David Stewart at William Grant, Richard Paterson at Whyte & Mackay, David Robertson at Macallan and Jim McEwan, ex of Bowmore and then resuscitating Bruichladdich. I approached all four and asked, 'How would you feel about tasting three hundred whiskies for me? And tasting them blind and rating them according to a list of flavours?' All, to my surprise, said yes, though they were all busy men.

I then took the project to my friends at the Scotch Whisky Research Institute. This is an outfit which had been set up by the brand owners to provide a solid scientific basis for what by then was Scotland's most important industry. The Institute was enthusiastic, provided I got the participation of the brand owners. Being assured of this, they provided the scientific underpinning of the project.

Frances Jack was my main contact there and she could not have been more helpful. She was enthusiastic about the idea of a definitive list of whisky flavours, as were several of her colleagues. They came up with the categories by which the *Directory* was to classify the flavours of all Scotch whiskies. They are: Floral, Fruity, Vanilla, Caramel, Nutty, Sweet, Smoky, Cereal, Aldehydic, Woody, Resinous, Sulphurous, Sour, Soapy and Musty. The presence of the first five is always pleasing, that of the middle five may be pleasant or not, depending on their strength relative to the first lot, the last five usually nasty, though tolerable in low concentrations. The whole thing is presented in a bar chart, with the flavours along the bottom and their intensity represented by the height of the bar. (It sounds complicated but is simple in practice.) The flavour of any whisky can be represented visually by this graphic.

I wrote to the proprietors of every Scotch whisky brand, telling them of the scheme and asking for a sample. I thought I might have difficulty obtaining some of the more obscure brands but was pleasantly surprised at the response. I had asked for twenty-five centilitre samples, which was the standard duty-free sample bottle. (At the time I was licensed by HMRC as a rectifier and could receive duty-free samples.) Some distillers sent proper certified samples, but the commonest response was someone phoning, saying, 'We don't have any samples to hand. Can we just send you a bottle?' Since the bottle would be duty-paid and I could legally drink what I didn't need, this was fine by me.

I bought over a thousand little sample jars and presented each of my tasters with about three hundred whiskies in those jars, together with a sheet for each jar, on which they had to enter the flavour they discerned in each whisky. (The *Directory* contained 265 entries; the balance was for controls. I'm pleased to say that the controls demonstrated remarkable consistency on the part of the tasters.) When they had tasted all their whiskies, my tasters returned the sheets to me and the people at the SWRI kindly crunched the numbers and came up with a balanced average for each flavour for each whisky, a big job.

The results were sometimes predictable and sometimes surprising, but I think this is not the place to comment (if you are sufficiently interested, I expect copies of the book can be found second-hand for it never ran to a second edition, which was disappointing). It was, however, a *succès d'estime*, and was approved by people whom I respected. Since I had had a lot of fun, it didn't matter that it didn't sell a million.

All this took place after I had been expelled from the Society as an undesirable influence by its careful management, so I needed a base for my researches. Some years earlier, our little yacht club in Granton had been given money by some quango to train kids in sailing. With some of the money they had bought two portacabins, which they sat in the boatyard, one on top of the other, with a stair up the front. The upper cabin hadn't been used for years, so I suggested to the club that I inhabit it while compiling the *Directory*. This I did, and spent a very happy year, perched high above Granton Harbour, with three hundred bottles of whisky and my boat at a mooring. I was very popular and had lots of visitors.

With the publication of the *Directory* I had said just about all I had to say about Scotch whisky. If you want to know what that was, find yourself a copy. But do be careful in your interpretation of its findings, it was published in 2005. Since things change over time and whisky is no exception, the flavour charts in the *Directory* can no longer be relied on as a guide to the flavour of the brands today. Those least likely to have changed are, I think, the blended whiskies, for consistency is at the heart of whisky blending. And the response to the book was not such as to make it likely that an updated edition will be forthcoming soon.

I have been told that I shall be expected to say something at this point about the present state of Scotch whisky and how the influence of the Society has manifested itself. Lacking as objective an assessment as an up-to-date *Directory*, I am a trifle reluctant to do this. But so long as it is understood that what follows is a subjective impression, I will venture the following. Let me begin with an illustration.

At Christmas last year, somebody gave me a bottle of malt whisky. I won't tell you the name of the distiller, which allows me to be as candid as I wish without giving offence. The bottle and label carry lots of symbols, all presumably implying high quality. The bottle, which is clear glass, has been cast with the name of the distillery and some small decorations. The labels (there are three) announce that it is single malt Scotch whisky and give the name of the island distillery, which is perfectly proper, together with the percentage alcohol (nearly 60%) and the information that the whisky has not been chill-filtered. They tell us that it is 'Small Batch', a designation borrowed from Bourbon producers who originally sought to emulate the Society, and which has never, to my knowledge, had application to whisky. It is Tuscan wine cask matured, which means, the back label tells us, that it has been in casks which previously held a red Tuscan wine. It was specially selected by a prominent retailer, though from what the selection was made it does not say, and is signed by a person who is described as a master distiller. The whisky has a light reddish colour. There is no age statement.

If I tell you that whisky doesn't stay long on the shelf in our house and that this stuff has been around for some months, you may be able to form some estimate of the value of the above information in regard to the excellence or otherwise of the whisky. And this, I think, illustrates something which ought to be of concern to the people who make and sell our whiskies. So long as the tides of fashion are running in favour of Scotch, it will be possible to sell stuff like this. But when the tide turns, I fear it will leave this one dry. My concern is that it will strand many others who less deserve the fate. Remember that the expansion of Scotch single malts was into the vacuum left when Cognacs imploded; today there are large stocks lying in Cognac of excellent quality which can find no buyers.

Let us, however, look a little more closely at our bottle, at what it says and what it leaves unsaid. Of the latter, the age statement or, rather, lack of it is surely significant. We all know that whisky requires to be matured in cask for many years if it is to acquire a desirable flavour. In this case a relatively new distillery is bringing to market a spirit which, while within the law governing such things, is much too young. No doubt it does so out of a laudable concern to make a return on its investment. On this showing, it does so by prejudicing its sales when its spirit shall become mature.

I found interesting the implication that a few years in a cask which previously held Tuscan red wine must necessarily produce good whisky. We are told on the back label that it was good Tuscan wine, which is a relief. (I have drunk a lot of Tuscan wine and I can tell you that it is variable in quality.) What we don't know is whether being in a former Tuscan wine cask makes for good whisky in the first place. It may do, but I don't see any reason to suppose it shall any more than a vinegar cask, nor do I know of extended experiments which have demonstrated the result of such maturation over a sufficient period. Fortified wines such as sherry have characteristics which unfortified wines do not, which make them suitable for whisky. I would venture that this whisky does not demonstrate the desirability of the latter. Certainly its colour is not alluring.

That the maturation was a small batch of casks tells us little without information about the size of the casks used: were they quarters or puncheons? It would make a big difference, for maturation in the latter is slower by some orders of magnitude. The endorsement by a leading retailer is suspect since he would say that, wouldn't he? It also suggests that the distiller, lacking an endorsement from a more authoritative source, seeks that of a person who will be selling the stuff and it must, *ipso facto*, be suspect.

I could go on, but this is becoming tedious. It is difficult to avoid the impression that the information given about this whisky is directed at the ignorant or – worse – the half-educated: people who have heard or read about the matters covered by the descriptions but without understanding. My concern is not for the makers of this whisky, it is for the many firms which do understand such things and employ their understanding to make really fine whisky. It is also that the understanding of maturation, which the Society first introduced into the public marketplace, is being misused. You may argue that we were to some extent to blame for bringing such things to light in the first place, but this is like blaming the inventor of the wheel for road accidents.

Another obvious malign consequence of what we did is to be found in any big airport duty-free. There, uncomprehending customers are seduced to buy wildly expensive whiskies by glossy packaging more appropriate to the adjacent perfume counter. Some of the whiskies are what they say they are: very fine and, in a world where scarcity makes for costliness, understandably dear. But quite a lot of the bottles on offer are not what the advertising implies them to be and must, to any discerning customer, be a source of disappointment. Brand owners should look along the shelf at the few similar Cognac bottles and draw a lesson.

The fact is, some people will do whatever makes them a shilling, often with little thought for whether another shilling may be got tomorrow, and the profits made by the cowboys are at the long-term expense of the good and careful whisky brands. The legislation which laid down the permissible materials and the necessity of cask maturation for spirit to be called Scotch Whisky is being stretched by unscrupulous operators to the detriment of the industry as a whole and it is high time the

Scottish Government gave the matter its attention. The pursuit of profit is the driver of this, as in any other industry, but it is surely the business of government to regulate to ensure that present pursuit does not prejudice future prospect.

CHAPTER 26

Bringing It Home

There came a time when we decided to move out of Edinburgh. We found, quite by accident, a lovely house in a village not far south of Aberdeen. The house was perfect. Besides the usual offices it had a wood, a stream, a pond and, in a boggy bottom, the remains of a Pictish church. It also had a stable block, which I occupied as a workshop. For Maggie, it provided closeness to her work, which was in Scotland's oil industry, and for me, congenial company in a nearby fishing village, where the harbourmaster was a friend of mine. It was a relationship based – as were so many of my friendships – on a liking for old boats, diesel engines, strong drink and philosophical discourse. My interest in olfactory matters sat well with all those topics, though it was something of a mystery to my companions. That said, they were prepared to listen when I descanted on the flavours of Scotch whisky, especially if I provided the whisky.

The perception of aroma is innate in almost all of us, a relic of the most primeval sensory organ of our amoeboid ancestors. It is at its most intense in childhood, which is why the most effective evokers of early memories are commonly smells. But for most people it declines with age, this diminution being the effect of two causes: the natural decay of the equipment and the lack of its exercise. Of the two, the latter is the more important, for the more you use it, the more likely you are to retain it. This was brought home to me in a way which, years later, I still wonder about. For smells can be profoundly mysterious, and they are sometimes very difficult to explain. First, let me set the scene.

Natural harbours are few on Scotland's east coast. For hundreds of years, only the Dutch took an interest in the fish which teemed in our coastal waters, and the lack of harbours didn't much matter. But when, for various reasons, the shoals of herring and cod began to be exploited in the nineteenth century, the lack of refuges for boats became acute. In the summer of 1848 there was a great storm in which half the fishing fleet was lost, and this impelled Queen Victoria's government to do something about it. That something – *pace* neoliberal economists – consisted of government money, channelled via the gentlemanly British Fisheries Society, into the building of decent harbours. An important industry was spawned which employed thousands of people and fed millions.

The results of this intervention are still visible – and mostly still useable – today, in the form of mighty stone harbour walls and breakwaters. Johnshaven was a beneficiary of the largesse. There had been a tiny settlement around a small cleft in the rocky coast, up which small boats could be drawn. The cleft was blasted to form a narrow channel and a harbour of refuge built complete with gate to protect against storm surge. Behind the harbour a substantial village grew up, in time sufficient to warrant a railway line. The village prospered for more than a century until, with the decline of the inshore fleet and the big-boat technology of distant-water fishing, its cottages became home to commuters and the retired. The harbour remains, though, and a harbour needs a harbourmaster. That was my chum Richard.

We had been brought together by a common interest. Not so common an interest really, for we were among the few people in the country – in the world, for that matter – who admired old Kelvin diesel engines. I had come across him while raking the country for bits for the J4 which I was rebuilding for the *Clan Gordon*; some guys I knew in Troon had told me of him and I had in consequence paid a visit to Johnshaven. Down by the harbour I had enquired as to the whereabouts of the harbourmaster, and been told that he was to be found in the Anchor, a pub all of twenty metres from the harbour wall. I found him. He was slight, stooped, balding and his dress would have been rejected by a charity shop. In another age his cough would have marked him for a consumptive.

In the pub, a dispute was in process of resolution. It seems that there had been a disagreement about who should berth his boat where, and the disputants had brought the matter before designated authority. The latter, who plainly knew a thing or two about conflict management, had begun by buying pints for the complainants. He listened solemnly to their representations and then, with a gravity which Socrates would have envied, delivered his judgement.

'Aye, lads, I can see ye have a problem. But it's no much of a problem. Just you sort it oot for yersels.'

This was not, as perhaps it might seem, an abnegation of responsibility, but a democratic conferring of onus upon the shoulders of the disputants themselves. It did not derogate from authority, it enhanced it. As far as I know, things settled down and there were no bad feelings: certainly I recall later that day seeing the parties to the dispute in a condition which required them to provide mutual support and navigation sufficient to find their respective homes.

Richard was a man of some importance in the village. Not

only was he the harbourmaster, he was the boatbuilder. On the waterfront, at the foot of the hill, was a small church. The village, which had once been pious enough to support several quite exotic varieties of religion, had abandoned the church years before. Richard had bought it for next to nothing and its nave became a boatshed. It had been in use for this purpose for a decade or two when first I made its acquaintance. Woodworking machines were arranged along the walls, among a truly vast number of miscellaneous articles of more-or-less maritime function which might, one day, come in handy. None of the machines appeared to have a safety guard of any sort. At the door, which had been cut in one of the long walls, stood a mighty bandsaw. The floor, which was rarely visible, was covered with wood shavings and sawdust, as were all the machines not currently in use. Because the premises were owned by an individual who had no employees, they were not subject to inspection by Health and Safety officials – which was probably just as well for the health and safety of the officials.

Along both walls ran central-heating radiators of miscellaneous design, evidently the ejecta of local home improvers. (The coast is a cold, windy place in winter and frozen fingers do not go well with sharp-edged tools.) But the glory of the central-heating system was the boiler. It had begun its life a century or more before as the vertical boiler of a steam engine. It stood about three metres high and its chimney went up through the roof. The whole thing was massively made of wrought iron and it was fed through an iron door near its foot. For food it used anything remotely combustible, of which there was no shortage, given that the floor was entirely composed of highly combustible wood shavings. Beside the fire door stood a big box marked with warning symbols. I had paid no notice to the box until one cold morning I happened by the church just as Richard was beginning his day. It was very cold. Richard shivered, dropped his cigarette end among the shavings, lit another and reached into the box. From it he pulled two big parachute flares. (These are distress flares. If it is night and you desperately need a lifeboat, you hold one in your right hand and pull the tag on the bottom with the left. After a few seconds it fizzes and then shoots a ball of red flame far into the night sky. The flare burns for several minutes.) Richard pulled the tags on both the flares, threw them into the boiler's firebox and slammed the door. There was a pause and then two dull, but massive, thumps and the whole boiler shook. 'That's fine,' he said, 'we'll soon get some heat.' It appears he had spent a year or two working for a company which supplied such things and disposed of them when they had passed their use-by date. Since the disposal cost money, they paid no attention when the out-of-date flares went missing.

About once a year Richard built a boat. He was limited by the size of the church to boats of about ten metres in length, but otherwise there were few restrictions on what he might build. Since there were no customers until a boat had been built, he could please himself as to its design. (It was known to be a bad idea to commission a boat from him. Since an advance order required, by convention, a payment up front, and work was unlikely to begin until the payment had been converted into potable form, word got around.) The boats tended to be of traditional build: keel of elm or oak, frames of oak and planks of larch, the planking to be either carvel or clinker. Richard preferred clinker (in which planks overlap and the watertightness of the hull depends on the precision of the overlap), I think because it required the greater skill. To anyone interested in smells, the church was a place of wonder. Each timber had a distinctive odour and there were, besides, the smells of oil and tar, and rope and paint, and fish.

One day I happened into the boatshed. Richard was there with his friend Lloyd and an older man. The three were gazing intently at a board of wood: a piece a couple of feet long by one deep. One of them had a pencil with which he was making marks on the wood. There would then be a discussion and another would take a turn of the pencil. I edged round, so that I could see what was going on without disturbing them. They were drawing the outline of a boat. With each alteration they would discuss how the change in shape would affect her motion in different sorts of sea conditions. All three were drawing on a lifetime's experience to design a weatherly, sea-kindly hull. When the discussion was over, Richard nailed the board on the wall, where it became the blueprint for the new boat.

It's taking a while to get back to the subject of olfactory perception, but bear with me.

Richard had a collection of ancient diesel engines, all Kelvins, which he kept in a disused cottage. He picked them up whenever he found one – in those days nobody wanted such things and their only cash value was as scrap iron. Each boat Richard built would be equipped with engine bearers suitable for a Kelvin and when it neared completion, an engine would be assembled out of the parts available. The engines would always run, though Richard's skills did not run to fine engineering. In this matter he was fortunate in his friend Graham. Graham was small, wiry, grizzled and Glaswegian. His origins were evident as soon as he spoke, for folk from Glasgow rarely lose the lilting tones which, I suspect, their ancestors brought from their native Highlands. Graham was a cheerful sort of fellow; his ready grin evidence both of his general disposition and his tendency to find humour in the actions of his fellows: with Richard he had no shortage of material. He was a peerless engineer and his depth of understanding was matched by his practical skills. I count it among the better aspects of my life that I have known a few people like Graham.

When I moved to that part of the world, my current boat, the *Clan Gordon*, had to come too. My friend Maxwell and I sailed her up over a couple of mild days that year. She performed perfectly, the great sail drawing beautifully in the light breezes and the engine, when required, starting without a cough. And when, late in the day, on a falling tide and a southerly breeze we tried to find the channel into the harbour mouth, there were Richard and Graham on the pier head signalling to us which way to steer.

The *Clan Gordon* was a west coast boat: her deep draught unsuited to east coast harbours, where she would dry out twice a day. When, one day, some fool removed the bridle which held her upright against the quay, she fell over and sat on a stone which penetrated her hull. It was a major emergency as we fought to stop the rising tide from swamping her. We lost that battle, but it was almost worth it for the memory of Richard and Graham at midnight, up to their knees in mud as they tried to fother her bottom against the rising water. We had some floodlights, which was just as well. We also had the police, the coastguard and numerous villagers who happily left their soap operas to be of assistance. Only once did we have a complaint, from a miserable couple who crept from their bijou waterside cottage to whine about the noise at three in the morning. They threatened to call the police, at which I took them along the quay to the local sergeant who gently explained to them that this was the sort of thing that sometimes happened in a harbour because it had boats in it, and if they didn't like it they might think about moving house. They had barely retreated when we were joined by other cottagers, recent incomers from somewhere in southern England. Far from complaining, they produced vacuum flasks full of hot tea, and sandwiches in case we were hungry.

The boat sank. Next day we brought in another of the villagers, who owned an enormous travelling crane, and lifted her out in front of an audience of the entire, delighted, village. Within hours, Graham had drained the engine, refilled it with oil and fired it up. The boat recovered, but not without extensive repair.

As an alliance, Richard and Graham were formidable. Their enthusiasms were irresistible and when they had a project in hand, the whole village knew about it. They both ran the same sort of motor car: a tiny Vauxhall, probably the smallest diesel-engined car on the market. Some years ago, some officious fool said in public what every diesel engineer knew, namely that you could run a diesel on any oil which had the requisite characteristics of viscosity and flash point. The stuff you fed a diesel didn't have to come out of a garage pump, it could come from anywhere provided it met those and a few other criteria. The legality of using such fuel on the road was another matter, but for a while nobody worried much about that.

You might have thought that neither Graham nor Richard would have been interested, given that they already got eighty miles to the gallon of fuel, and neither did that much driving. But you would have been wrong – they adopted the idea, rejoicing. They had a friend in the next village along the coast, who owned a fish and chip shop. They applied to the friend, saying that they might, without charge, relieve him of some of his redundant frying oil. Since a chipper has to pay to get rid of old, no longer usable oil, the friend complied and my chums acquired a large quantity of the stuff. They contrived a filter and Graham made whatever adjustments he thought appropriate to injectors and pumps. Naturally, the whole village knew about it.

Now, dear reader, dear, *patient* reader, no doubt you are wondering what this has to do with olfactory perception. It is this. When the two drove through the village, everyone could smell fish and chips. You may say that after being first vaporised and then burnt at high pressure in the cylinder of a diesel engine, no chip oil could retain the aroma of things which were fried in it months before. I can tell you it did, though I cannot begin to imagine the chemistry. But there is an even greater mystery: when they drove past, I swear, I *swear* I could smell vinegar.